Animal
Magic

Also by Gordon Smith
and published by Hay House

Books

Mediumship (2017)

The Unbelievable Truth (2004, 2005, 2015)

Positive Vibes (2013)

Intuitive Studies (2012)

Developing Mediumship (2009)

Why Do Bad Things Happen? (2009)

Spirit Messenger (2008)

Life-Changing Messages (2007)

Through My Eyes (2007)

Stories from the Other Side (2006)

Audio Programs

Developing Mediumship with Gordon Smith (2007)

The Healing Power of Mediumship (2006)

*Gordon Smith's Introduction to the Spirit World:
A Live Lecture* (2006)

Online Courses

Introduction to Mediumship (2017)

Animal Magic

*The Extraordinary Proof of Our Pets' Intuition
and Unconditional Love for Us*

#1 *Bestselling Author*
GORDON SMITH

HAY HOUSE

Carlsbad, California • New York City
London • Sydney • New Delhi

First published in the United Kingdom by:
Hay House UK Ltd, The Sixth Floor, Watson House,
54 Baker Street, London W1U 7BU
Tel: +44 (0)20 3927 7290; Fax: +44 (0)20 3927 7291
www.hayhouse.co.uk

Published in the United States of America by:
Hay House Inc., PO Box 5100, Carlsbad, CA 92018-5100
Tel: (1) 760 431 7695 or (800) 654 5126; Fax: (1) 760 431 6948 or (800) 650 5115
www.hayhouse.com

Published in Australia by:
Hay House Australia Ltd, 18/36 Ralph St, Alexandria NSW 2015
Tel: (61) 2 9669 4299; Fax: (61) 2 9669 4144; www.hayhouse.com.au

Published in India by:
Hay House Publishers India, Muskaan Complex, Plot No.3, B-2,
Vasant Kunj, New Delhi 110 070
Tel: (91) 11 4176 1620; Fax: (91) 11 4176 1630; www.hayhouse.co.in

Text © Gordon Smith, 2008, 2018

Previously published as *The Amazing Power of Animals* (ISBN: 978-1-84850-008-2)

A catalogue record for this book is available from the British Library.

ISBN: 978-1-4019-7299-8

Interior images: 67b, 211b Shutterstock; 197b Gordon Smith;
211t Trevillion Images; all other images 123RF

Printed in the United States of America

To all the wonderful animals included in this book. For the tremendous joy, love, compassion and teachings they gave.

To Sassie — a very special wee lassie. And Izzy, Chris and Nancy should know that she sleeps happy in heaven.

To Tiger, a cat with attitude. And who could forget Lassie, a dog who made looking good an art form. A true companion, that was Rosie. To big fat Elsa, who always made us laugh, and to gentle Cindy for loving my boys so much.

A special big kiss to Miss Meg — a love-hound who kept us all entertained.

For all those involved in 'The Animal Service' over the years.

To Charles, the third Earl of Fluffington — more commonly known as CHEEKY CHARLIE. I just know you're causing trouble in heaven.

MAY ALL BEINGS BE HAPPY.

Contents

Acknowledgements

To Susanna Forest, thank you once again for your great work on this book.

To Lizzie Hutchins, perfect once again.

A special thank you to Jo Lal for making this book happen.

To Jo Burgess for the many nights helping me sort the world out.

To Michelle Pilley and everyone at Hay House for all your hard work and belief in what I do.

Introduction

If you look around you, it seems as though every day there's an extraordinary story in the media that makes you marvel at the intuition and compassion of animals. In this book I'd like to tell you some of the stories I've come across in my many years of working as a medium and to answer some of the questions people ask about animals. These are in fact very similar to the questions I'm asked about humans. Do animals live on in spirit? Can they send us signs through a medium or do something else to make us aware of their presence, like moving a favourite toy or brushing past us? Will they be there to greet us when we pass?

I can't make a connection with everyone's pet, but I try to reassure these people that of course the answer to all these questions is a resounding 'Yes!' Just like humans, animals cannot die for the life of them. They too go to the spirit world. I've lost count of the number of readings I've given where an animal has been there, sitting alongside a person who's recently passed, a companion in death as in life.

For me as a medium, the experience of bringing through an animal is just the same as making a connection to a human spirit: I feel a presence, a personality that is impressed on me, I see images and I feel a real, palpable emotional connection that affects the owners too. Just as I know if a human spirit is happy, I can tell when a dog or cat is content and wants to let its owners know that they shouldn't worry about it.

The spirit world is actually a different level of consciousness, a level that's more illuminated, where a being can see further and more clearly than they did on Earth. So animals who are there can still be aware of what's going on in our lives and offer support, just as they do in this world.

The following story, from a friend of mine called Sue, who is an animal healer, highlights the magic that can occur when people have a genuine loving bond with animals. I will let her tell you in her own words what happened:

> I had been asked to give healing to a lovely chestnut thoroughbred horse called Dexter. His owner, Beth, told me she had been riding him for many years with no problems and over the last year her daughter, Katy, had also started to ride him. Dexter was such a gentle and reliable horse that Beth was sure Katy would be safe on his back, and at first they had worked fine together. Katy had become interested in doing dressage and they had won a few shows, and Beth had been pleased to see Katy starting to get a passion for all things horsey, just as she had. So it came as a big surprise to her when Dexter started to behave rather strangely when Katy rode him out.

I asked Katy to tell me exactly what had been happening.

'I get on Dexter's back and we trot out into the field,' she said, 'then after about 10 minutes of us cantering around, he suddenly stops dead and just stands there, as if he doesn't want to walk on any further. Then he rears up and then just stands there again, and I get off and try to get him to walk forward, or sideways, or try and pull him along, but he won't budge. After a few minutes, he just walks on and is fine again, so I get back on him and we start riding round again, and he's okay for a while, but then he stops and does the whole thing all over again. It's so frustrating.'

Beth added, 'We have his feet checked and reshod on a regular basis, so it's not that, and I've had the vet out to look him over, and he said he couldn't find anything wrong and he didn't think he was in any pain. I can't understand it, as I still ride him and I don't get these problems.'

I love horses, so I was happy to help. I went to Dexter in his stable and let him sniff and snuffle me. Then I reached up and placed my hands on his big strong shoulders and tuned in to him. Everything felt fine to me. His coat was smooth and his eyes were clear. He was a beautiful creature and I wasn't picking up anything that led me to think he was ill or in pain physically, but I asked for healing to be channelled to him anyway, as this couldn't do any harm.

As I carried on tuning in to him, in my mind's eye I saw a girl of about 14 in what looked like a school. I realized it was Katy, and she was being picked on by girls of a similar age. Had Dexter been aware of her fear and negative feelings about this when she rode him, I wondered. I then felt he was *showing me what he'd been trying to convey to Katy through his strange behaviour: by standing firm he was saying that Katy had to stand her ground with the other girls, and by rearing up, he was indicating that she had to stand up for herself. I was also picking up the loving and protective feelings he had for both Katy and Beth. What a fabulous horse he was. I conveyed to him that I would help them as best I could.*

I then asked Katy if she would take Dexter out of his stable into the field and see if she could show me what they normally did, but with one difference. 'When you're riding Dexter,' I said, 'I want you to remember some of your happiest times — like when you opened your presents at Christmas or when you got your first pony. Just try and conjure up that sort of feeling. If anything not so nice comes into your mind, just ignore it and go back to the nice thoughts. And from now on, whenever you take Dexter out to ride, I want you to think only of those happy times, okay?'

'Okay,' she answered, 'but if I do that, who will I talk to about my problems in the future? I've got lots of happy memories, but Dexter knows about them already. What about any other stuff that's going on, and what if I've got nothing good to tell him?'

'So you already talk to Dexter about everything?' I said.

'Yeah, of course I do,' she replied. 'Not always out loud — in my head mostly — but I share everything with you, don't I, Dex?'

She patted his head.

It was all starting to make sense to me now. Dexter had become her confidant and she'd been offloading all of her problems and negative emotions onto the poor chap.

I watched her ride him around the field, up and down, round and round, and each time they passed me, I shouted, 'Happy thoughts, Katy! Don't forget, happy thoughts!'

When they'd been going round for over 20 minutes, I asked, 'Is that better?'

'He's been great,' she called back, 'he hasn't stopped once, he's been just like his old self.'

When they came past again, I said, 'Okay, Katy, can you get off him now, as I would like to have a little chat with you.'

We started to walk back to the house.

'I think your Dexter is a smashing horse,' I said, 'and I don't know if you realize it, but he's a very sensitive soul and I think what's been upsetting him these past few weeks is that maybe you've been having a few problems at school…? If I'm right, I think you should talk to your mum about it. What do you say?'

I wasn't sure how she would respond, as it was a delicate subject, and after all I was a stranger to her, but she blurted out straightaway, as if she needed to tell someone, 'I want to, but I can't! I don't want to upset my mum. We moved to this area just to get me into that horrid school, but I hate it, I hate it!'

Tears were welling up in her eyes.

'And everyone there hates me too,' she added.

'I'm sure that's not true,' I said quickly.

'Why not?' she asked. 'I don't seem to fit in, and there's this group of girls who pick on me.'

My heart went out to her. 'I understand what it can be like,' I said.

'How can you?' she snapped back at me.

'Well, I had a horrible time at school too,' I said.

She looked surprised.

'I was a tomboy,' I told her, 'and all I wanted to do was play football and look after animals. I didn't want to talk about boys non-stop and hang around the shopping centre after school, which is what the rest of the girls seemed to do. No one seemed to understand me either, and they'd give me a hard time, but after a while they got bored with picking on me and left me alone. That sort of thing can happen if you don't fit in with the rest of the crowd or if you're a bit different. But being bullied is a different matter altogether, and if that's what's happening to you, you must tell your mum about it. In either case, she wouldn't want you to be unhappy at school, would she? And Dexter certainly isn't happy about it, is he?'

'Is that why you asked me to think of good things when I rode Dexter?'

'Yes, I think Dexter has been picking up on your sadness and your problems at school, and now you've told me you've been telling him about your problems, it all makes sense. He has been concerned about you and, in his own way, he has been trying to tell you to stand firm and stand up for yourself.'

'He's my best friend,' she said thoughtfully, 'and I do tell him everything, but now I'll be more careful what I share with him. I'll try and remember to think happy thoughts when I'm riding him. It certainly helped today.'

'That's good,' I said. 'You can still talk to him about stuff, but just be aware that he may want to get involved and try and help you.'

'He's such an old Mother Hubbard!' she said, her mood lightening a bit, and we both laughed.

'Animals are really sensitive and do pick up on our feelings, both positive and negative,' I explained.

Katy went back to the stables and I went back to the house to have a chat with her mum.

Beth wasn't aware that her daughter was having problems with the other girls at school and said she would have a chat with her later, and that if Katy needed to change schools, then she would do her best to make that happen. She was relieved to hear that I hadn't picked up anything negative health-wise with Dexter and that he had only been acting strangely out of concern for Katy.

'Yeah, but be careful what you two tell him in future,' I joked, *'as he's not very good at keeping secrets! Thankfully...'*

It was a privilege for me to be of some help, but I believe Dexter was the real healer that day. Animals have so much love and wisdom to share with us and all we have to do is be open to it.

This story really lifts me up each time I tell it to people, as it reminds me of how the animals that love us are affected by our emotions. I wonder how many people who have pets off-load their problems onto them when they are alone with them? This story might give you a little more insight into how your animals feel when you dump your emotional baggage on them. Keep talking to them by all means, but remember they can feel what you feel, even if they can't always display it back to you.

This case also shows that Sue is an amazing animal sensitive and healer, and Dexter displays extraordinary abilities in transmitting his feelings through clairvoyant images. It's actually quite magical.

I have experienced the magic of animals in my own life. In particular I've known and loved many wonderful dogs. My beautiful Miss Meg, for example, a lovely springer spaniel, could find anything she was asked to with her keen nose. Even after she passed away in January 2016, she found something for me from her vantage point in the spirit world.

It was two months after losing Meg that I was walking in the open countryside where I live with Cookie, my other springer, and suddenly lost my footing and fell over. The ground was frozen, but fortunately I didn't hurt myself. After dusting myself off, I carried on walking for a bit and then, when I put my hand in my coat pocket, I noticed that I'd lost my house keys, which had a fob attached for the electric gate.

I called out to Cookie, who was way ahead of me, to come back, and started to retrace my steps in order to find the keys, which I assumed would be lying near where I'd fallen. It was easy for me to identify the spot, as some of the long grass was flattened, but I couldn't see the keys anywhere. After searching for 10 minutes or so, I gave up, as the cold weather was really starting to bite, but marked the spot so that I could try again the following day.

I walked the same way every day and I knew that no one else used the route, so I was confident that I would find the keys. The annoying thing was that I only had two fobs for the gates, one of which was now lost, and that type of fob was no longer made, so if I couldn't recover it, I'd have to spend a lot of money and change the whole mechanism.

Every day I searched at the spot where I'd fallen. I pulled the grass and reeds in every direction, but found nothing. Soon I was considering changing the electric gates, fearing that if my only other fob went on the blink it would cause me a lot of trouble.

It must have been a month later that one of my sons suggested letting Cookie sniff the remaining fob and setting him off on a mission to find the other one. But this added up to nothing, for Cookie was hopeless as a sniffer dog. Whatever he was asked to find, he just chased pheasants and grouse around the moors.

As a last-ditch effort, I turned to my friend Robbie, who was walking with me that morning, and said, 'Okay, we're going to have to ask Miss Meg to find the keys for us.'

We both laughed and walked on over the rough terrain and up to the top of a nearby hill, which was actually where we had scattered our beloved Meg's ashes.

As we approached this beautiful site, we both suddenly noticed that hanging on a long reed were my keys. They were nowhere near where I'd fallen – in fact they were about a quarter of a mile further up the rugged hillside – and we had no idea how they could have got there. If a person had found them, they might have left them on a fence post, but not a thin reed. Also, no one else had come that way, as there wasn't a path other than the thin line where our own footsteps had made a slight dent in the reeds and long grass.

There could only be one explanation: we both laughed out loud and called out our thanks to the fabulous Miss Meg! I don't care what anyone else makes of this account, I'm sure my princess Meg somehow led us to where those keys were.

Not to be outdone, Cookie also found something that morning, which he brought to us with great pride. It was the half-eaten carcass of a rotting old pheasant. Never mind, maybe we still have time to teach a new dog old tricks...

For those of us who love animals, the world is all the more fantastic and often the more beautiful for it. I believe that the deeper consciousness of our animals carries a magical quality that we can learn more about. There is much more to our amazing pets and their magic than we have yet discovered...

CHAPTER ONE

My Animals and Other Family

It's funny to think that I really had a country childhood, even though I spent the first 14 years of my life in a terraced house in Springburn, to the north of Glasgow. It was an ordinary working-class neighbourhood, but I only had to walk for 10 minutes or so to get to Springburn Park, which was huge, with fields and patches of woodland and ponds with all kinds of birds like grebes, ducks and swans.

If you went 20 minutes further on to Torrance, you found a stretch of marsh at the foot of some hills, and as the land rose it turned into heathland covered in heather and gorse bushes with their yellow flowers and sharp thorns. I used to call this place 'the pheasant fields', because it was full of the beautiful red birds. It was paradise. I could spend hours out there with my friends or my brothers and sisters. Our mum would boot us out of the front door and tell us to keep busy and out of trouble, and we'd head straight for the fields. It was unfarmed, and the higher you went, the closer you came to the Campsie Hills, where there was even more wildlife. It was the most magical place to play.

What did we do? I suppose we were just watching, really, entranced by the natural world unfolding in front of our eyes. Often it would be pitch black by the time we realized we should head home. That would be the only reason we knew it was teatime – the light was gone!

There were endless hours of discoveries. Within a very short space of time I had built up a vast knowledge of animals and birds, all because I was there to watch things as they happened – a blue tit building a nest twig by twig, or a wren singing, or a woodpecker tapping into a tree. It was fascinating to see how a bird camouflaged itself or disputed its territory, and it was great food for the mind. Nowadays if you want to know something you just Google it, but there's nothing like the experience of actually being there and watching nature develop. We could follow a family of birds from the courtship of the parents to the nest building, the egg hatching and the first flight of the baby birds. Once we watched curlew chicks hatching from their eggs. I must have been about 12 at the time. An adult curlew was running along the ground, pretending it had a broken wing. That's what these birds do to distract predators from their chicks. We only had to go a short way to find the nest and the speckled eggs with the long curlew beaks pecking through, and soon the grey and black fluffy chicks tumbled out. Then, once every chick was hatched, they suddenly ran in all directions for cover.

The biggest thrill was seeing a sparrowhawk or a hen harrier hovering high over the bracken and preparing to plunge down and seize some poor little creature as prey. I also loved to stand as close as I dared to a deer without it flinching or running away – I learned that if I kept my head down and didn't 'confront' the animals, they wouldn't be afraid of me. I read up on what I saw, too, and I was proud that I knew the Latin name of every bird species in Britain by the time I was 12.

Going out into the natural world was the greatest joy for us as kids. We never got bored. Sometimes we would catch a bus and get right out into open countryside or visit a loch. Occasionally we would rescue some of the casualties or abandoned baby birds we found and bring them home to try and raise them as pets. Unfortunately, my mum couldn't stand animals. She'd been attacked by a cat when she was a girl and that had put her off them. Besides, as the mother of seven kids with four younger brothers and sisters of her own to look after, she just thought that having an animal around the house meant even more work and her day was short enough already. So she wouldn't let us have any pets, but the thing was, she never went out into the far reaches of the backyard where we had a hut. So we ran our animal hospital there.

It was quite a neighbourhood attraction. All the kids in the street knew that our mum didn't approve, so when they came round and knocked on the front door and she asked them who they were calling for, they'd look her straight in the eye and name one of us, and she'd send them out to the backyard to find us.

In the hut and in the sheds and pens we built we had all sorts of creatures: a seagull with a broken wing, a rabbit we'd had from a baby, a ferret someone had given us because they didn't want it any more, magpies that had fallen out of the nest, a hedgehog, a stray tortoise... We even dug out a pond for one resident – a perch, which the seagull later ate. One of the longest-serving residents was a cat called Tiger that we even used to sneak into the house when my mum was out at the shops or with the neighbours.

My dad loved animals – that's where we got our love of them from. He knew about the animal hospital and used to turn a bit of a blind eye when we smuggled Tiger into the house. Tiger knew all about Mum anyway – as soon as she got near the house he'd shoot out of the door and we'd all know she was coming!

In the end there was one animal that melted Mum's heart. I'm not sure if we found her or if she found us, but Lassie was a very special dog from the start. A gang of us had all taken the bus out to Lumloch near Springburn one day to tramp around and watch the wildlife. I must have been about 10 years old. Out of nowhere a beautiful red setter appeared, with an amazing auburn-coloured long silky coat and brown eyes. She joined in our walk as if it was the most natural thing in the world and we threw sticks for her and made a fuss of her. She looked like a pedigree show dog, not your run-of-the-mill mutt, and we just assumed that she'd lost her owners temporarily while she was out for a walk or that she lived nearby and was just out and about that day, keeping herself entertained. At the end of the day she'd probably take herself home, we reckoned.

The end of the day came and we were kicking our heels at the bus stop, but she wouldn't leave. 'Come on, girl, time to go back to your home,' but no, she wouldn't budge, just kept on wagging her tail as if it were all a game. We waved and shooed her and she still wouldn't go. She singled me out especially, keeping just by my heels. As the sky began to darken the bus pulled up – one of those old-fashioned Routemasters with the open platform at the back – and we climbed on and headed home, leaving the dog behind. Or so we thought. We were sitting up on the top deck when the setter's head popped up over the railings, her ears pricked and her tongue lolling out of her mouth as if to say, 'Found you!'

We decided that if she was coming with us, well, she'd just have to, and when we got back we'd report her to the police. She trotted happily down the street after us and greeted my dad like a long-lost friend. He admired her, but told us we'd have to let the police know where she was. 'She's too good a dog to be a stray. I expect someone's missing her.' He rang up the local station and reported Lassie as found, and they promised they'd get word out and see if anyone had reported a red setter bitch missing. Or at least, that's what he told us. Nowadays I have a sneaking suspicion that he wanted a dog so much that he never told the police at all!

Either way, the next day no one from the station rang. No one rang that week or the week after. Soon a month had gone by and no one had claimed Lassie, as we'd decided to name her. She was still living in the shed or the yard at that point and Mum was making ominous noises about giving her away if no one claimed her soon.

Lassie had singled me out as her favourite person in the house and at night she'd sneak into the house and up into my room, nose her way under the covers and sleep there. She liked to lie next to the wall, her legs braced against it so she took up half the bed and I was nearly pushed out onto the floor. My mum would come in to see me sometimes and catch her there, haul her out and send her packing. It didn't seem to bother Lassie that much, though – she was such a good-natured dog, she never held a grudge.

She was a beautiful dog, full of that red-setter elegance and totally sweet-natured. In the end my mum let her stay in the house and one day she even stroked her, and we all knew what a gesture that was for her. Mum even joked that Lassie was a reincarnation of her own dad, who used to sleep in what became my room before he died. He'd been a redhead and Lassie used to huff and puff whenever she was there, just as he had. She taught my mum how to love animals.

She didn't only love us humans, she was very generous with her affections all round, and she had litter after litter of mongrels by every mutt in the neighbourhood! We always found good homes for them. She came with us to the pheasant fields, and the moors too, and loved to dive into the river Kelvin and swim after the swans.

Sadly, when I was 14 we moved out of the terraced house and into a flat nearer the city centre in the Gorbals where my mum, dad and two of my brothers worked. We couldn't keep Lassie or any of the other pets in the animal hospital once we moved. Lassie went to live with one of my older brothers who had a house in the suburbs. He was unable to keep her at home, so eventually she moved next door to him to live on a farm and have the run of the fields. I visited her as often as I could.

One morning when I was 18 I woke up with tears streaming down my face. I just had an overwhelming feeling of emptiness and the sense that something was missing. By that point I'd started to have very strong gut feelings about things that later turned out to be true. I associated this sense of loss with Lassie automatically, so I wasn't at all surprised when later that day my brother phoned and told my mum Lassie had suddenly fallen ill and been put down. I was gutted.

I didn't have another dog until I was married to Katie and we had our two sons, Steven and Paul. The first dog was a springer spaniel that only lasted a day because it was just too mental to trust with the kids. Then we had a big black furry collie from the cats' and dogs' home called Cindy. She was perfect with the boys – they could have done anything to her and she wouldn't have reacted; her nature was just golden. She was more Katie's dog, so when we separated Cindy stayed with her and she died when the boys were old enough to leave school.

The next dog I had was Elsa, whom my partner Jim and I inherited from his mother. She was a fat old golden Labrador with bad hips who didn't need much walking and was happy just to lounge around at home with a ball in her mouth while we were out at work. At the time we were living in a basement flat under the Spiritualist church and were busy with the community who met there.

One evening, 8 December 1995 in fact, we were sitting in the development circle in the Spiritualist church. That was where a group of us would gather together to meditate and try and clear our minds so we were opened up to spirit. My friend Dronma, a Tibetan Buddhist who's a psychic artist, had joined us and she was drawing some of the spirit people who were contacting us that night. When we had finished meditating and were sitting round talking about what we'd experienced, Dronma showed us her pencil sketches. She normally did seven or eight a session and often it was clear that they were of a relative or a loved one who'd passed. Sometimes nobody recognized the faces and when that happened Dronma would sign and date the sketches in case it later became clear what they meant; they were probably predictions which would make sense later. That night she flipped over a page and there was a drawing of a springer spaniel puppy sitting in front of a door.

'I don't know why I drew this at all,' she said. 'I don't think it's a spirit dog. Look behind it. That's your front door, Gordon.'

I had to wonder, but she was right – it did look like my front door. We all admired the sketch, which was full of detail – the pup had a white chest with lots of spots and a crooked white stripe down his nose.

'You should remember this,' Dronma said. 'It's just a pencil drawing, but his collar is blue and the little plastic barrel hanging from it is red.' Then she dated the drawing.

I didn't think any more about it, because we weren't looking to get another dog. There wasn't room and neither of us had the time because we were both working. The last thing we needed was a robust springer spaniel pup that required a couple of runs round the park every day. The pencil drawing was folded back into Dronma's sketchbook and we all went off for tea and sandwiches.

Nine months later I had a call from a clairvoyant called June Oakley, who was a friend. We often got in touch to swap stories and catch up with everything that had been going on. A couple of minutes into the conversation she suddenly broke off her train of thought and said, 'You're going to be offered another pup. He's got long ears and a beautiful face – he's ever so cute. When you see him you'll fall in love with him. I am being told by my friends in the spirit world that you must accept this little dog. You can't turn him down because he needs a home. He's been abused and he needs you.' She said that Albert Best, the brilliant Glasgow medium who had been a sort of mentor to me, was telling her that I should have this dog.

In spite of this, I didn't take her too seriously. 'Well, they'll have to find another home for it because there's no way I can have a dog just now, no matter what Albert says.' I didn't make the connection with the dog in Dronma's sketch.

June didn't push me, just said, 'Well, dear, that's what he said,' and we left it at that.

Another week passed and I was speaking at a Spiritualist seminar. When I'd finished, an elderly lady came up to me and asked if I knew anyone who would be willing to take in a dog. She was very agitated, telling me, 'He'll have to go back in the dogs' home if no one will have him. My upstairs neighbours have got him and they're out at work all day, so they just lock him in a cupboard. It's right above the cupboard in my flat and I can hear him howling away in there. I can't stand it, so I tell them I'll look after him a little, but he's terrified when he comes over and races around and messes all over the floor. I'm too old to cope with that, but I can't bear the poor wee thing to go back to the dogs' home again. This is the third time he's been rehomed and I'm sure they'll put him down if he goes back. He's not even a year old and he's had a hard time of it.'

I gently said it just wasn't possible, thinking of our little basement flat and the fact that we were both out working at the barber's shop all day, and she looked crestfallen.

As she turned to go, I remembered the conversation with June and I called out after her, 'Wait a minute. Is this dog a spaniel?'

She looked surprised. 'Yes, it is.'

'Can I come and see him? If he's friendly I might be able to take him home, but we don't really have the time to look after a problem dog. Give me your phone number and I'll talk to Jim.'

I went downstairs to the flat and found Jim. 'Do you remember that message June gave me about a dog? Someone's just asked if we'll give a spaniel a home and I think we ought to go and see him. He's a bit of a problem case, but that's what Albert told June.'

Jim wasn't very enthusiastic, because he'd had a springer when he was little and knew how much work they could be, but he said we might as well go and see the pup. Later that evening I phoned the lady and arranged to go and visit her the next Monday.

When we got to the flat there was this springer, not quite a pup but still very young, with long brown ears, a white chest covered with spots, a blue collar with a red plastic barrel hanging from it and a long tail which was wagging frantically. We sat down to have a cup of tea and take a look at him and he jumped up on the couch and snuck into Jim's lap, then climbed up and wrapped himself round his neck, sitting on top of his shoulders like a fur collar. He was a big dog to do that, but somehow he knew he had to win Jim over and he clung to him like a puppy.

After that, Jim loved him and I loved him too and that was that. We couldn't leave him there. He was such a sweet-natured dog, he couldn't be that badly behaved now, could he? We put him in the car and waved goodbye to the lady, who was absolutely delighted that the dog would be safe. He was excited in the car, pacing up and down the back seat and looking out of the window with his tail going like a whisk. 'It's all right now,' I told him. 'You're going to a good home.'

Within two minutes of being let into our flat he'd messed on the floor, mounted poor old Elsa, who had no idea what was going on, and was racing in and out of the rooms, grabbing things, shaking them and throwing them up in the air.

Jim looked at me and said, 'There is no way we can keep that dog. That dog is mental.'

I was busy trying to stop Charlie dragging the sheets off the bed, 'Och, he just needs time to settle down! He'll be all right in a day or two.'

'A day or two of this?'

'Albert Best,' I thought, as I grabbed one end of a pillow that the spaniel was killing, 'is this your idea of a joke?'

The funny thing, though, is that Charlie, aka Cheeky Charlie, really was ours right from the beginning. A month after we brought him home his papers arrived and as I glanced over them I noticed his birth date: 8 December 1995, the day that Dronma drew the little spaniel puppy with the spots on his chest and the blue collar with the red barrel, sitting on my doorstep. We tried to get him into a sitting position long enough to take a photo to match the pencil sketch and when we compared them the likeness was amazing — even the specks of brown on his chest were in the same position and the stripe on his nose was a perfect match.

Now I suppose if this were a fairy story this would be the point where it all ended happily ever after, with Charlie safe and happy with us. Destiny accomplished. Clearly we were meant to have him, but whoever it was in spirit who sent poor Charlie our way wanted us to learn some lessons from this new, boisterous and very damaged character. We really had our work cut out and our patience and compassion were tested to the limits.

From the very beginning Charlie was a challenge and an education. He wasn't 'just a dog', whatever that might be, he was a very special individual, but right from the start he was difficult. He'd had three different owners in nine months and it became clearer and clearer that he'd been very badly treated by some of them. We think his first owner had abused him and burned him with cigarettes and by the time the dogs' home had intervened he had become a scared and aggressive dog. The people at his second two homes hadn't known how to deal with him. Who knows what had been done to him as they tried to discipline him and knock the fear out of him?

Whatever the reason, the next three years were one long struggle for us. I knew that Jim was very houseproud and wouldn't stand for too much home wrecking by Charlie, so I found myself covering up for the dog and keeping the worst of his exploits from my partner. Pretty soon I had to change the whole pattern of my life to deal with this dog who had turned everything upside down.

He had every worst characteristic of a boy springer spaniel. As a breed they're known for their energy and intelligence, and Charlie managed to make the worst of both those traits. He chewed everything – our shoes, the furniture, the doors, the corners of carpets – and I couldn't hide that from Jim. You couldn't mend anything after he'd been at it. The things he destroyed were unbelievable – banknotes were a favourite. You daren't leave anything lying about. I'd bought Steven and Paul a game about vampires that was their pride and joy, but Charlie gnawed a hole straight through the middle of the hard-backed rule book and ate all the cards with the characters on them.

The first time we went out and left him home alone we came back and found he'd peed on the bed and ripped up the pillows. Whenever we came home from a trip to the shops or a night out without him, we had to brace ourselves for whatever surprise he'd cooked up while we were out.

I changed my shift so I worked mornings and Jim worked afternoons. We got up early and took him for a long run in the park before we left, to try and tire him out a little, and while we were at work we asked friends to pop in and feed him or take him out for a pee. They'd call me up and say, 'God, you should see the state of your house now,' and I'd have to beg them not to let on to Jim.

As soon as I'd finished with my last client I'd race back home, fling open the door and assess the wreckage. A lady came round to do the ironing for us once a week and Charlie would dig all the freshly pressed sheets and shirts out of the basket where she'd left them, toss them about, then roll all over them. I'd have to pick all the dog hair off the laundry and iron it all over again before Jim got back, then throw the sheets Charlie'd peed on into the washing machine and put some clean ones on the bed.

Once I got home and couldn't even open the door. I could hear Charlie barking away inside, but something was jamming the door firmly shut. I put my shoulder to it, but only managed to shove it open an inch or two. I wondered what on earth had happened. I shoved the door till it almost came off its hinges, but eventually I had to give up and go round to the back. The back door juddered when I opened it and I looked at the inside of it and realized that Charlie had managed to scratch right through the hardboard and into the cardboard lining – a little more work and he would have scraped through the hardboard on the other side and been running around the streets.

The living room was covered with clothes and there was a smell of fresh dog pee. Then I saw what had happened to the front door. Charlie had ripped the carpet up, nails and all, and rolled and rucked it up and wedged it like a log against the door. I couldn't hide that from Jim.

Another time Jim bought me some Harley Davidson boots for my birthday, which were pretty expensive, given what we could afford at the time, and I left them in their box in the living room overnight. I hadn't even tried them on. In the morning I found the box lid askew, but not completely off. 'Ah well,' I thought, 'Charlie can't have got at them, otherwise the lid would be on the other side of the room,' but when I lifted it off, there were the boots, still tucked up in tissue paper, only Charlie had poked his nose in and chewed off the tongues. How could I tell Jim? These had cost a fortune. I did my best to mend them with some Superglue and after that I only wore them under my jeans so the tops didn't show. Jim never noticed, but I didn't tell him till months later.

'If I'd have caught that dog!' he said.

'That's why I didn't tell you!'

One Christmas I presented one of Jim's sisters with a box of posh chocolates that had been sitting under the tree for a week or so with all the nicely wrapped gifts. She opened it up to offer it round and said to me, 'Ha, ha, very funny.' There wasn't a chocolate left in the box. Some time that week Charlie had nosed it open, hoovered out the sweeties and left the box there looking as though it hadn't been touched – and there he was, skulking behind the tree! He knew he was in the doghouse!

It was a really hard struggle to love Charlie. He was so bright and intelligent, though, and it was obvious he'd had a hard time. He didn't mind women at all, but if a man leaned over him he'd become aggressive and start barking and snapping. Jim'd act as the alpha dog and challenge him, 'nipping' him with his fingers when he growled or bit. I took a different view of it. Here was this dog who had never known anything but violence from humans – a lighted cigarette, a kick in the ribs. He had never been shown compassion and, like any sentient being who's never experienced that, his personality had been badly affected. I decided to show him that humans weren't his enemies and he didn't need to struggle for power with us. We needed him to trust us. So I did something that no dog whisperer would ever recommend: I let Charlie be the alpha dog. I'd lie on the floor and let him stand over me, pinning me down. He'd growl like a tiger, his nose so close to mine it was touching. He never bit me, though.

In fact, I only knew him be really hostile to someone twice. Once was to a junkie who had wandered into the church. Charlie seemed to know he was different from all the other people who were coming and going, and barked at him till he saw him off. The other time was to a person whom a lot of people seemed to have a problem with. Charlie wouldn't even let him in the house. On the whole, though, he just wanted human company, and that was the problem – being left alone with Elsa reminded him of being locked in that cupboard and deserted. No wonder he objected and took it out on the soft furnishings. When we went out and left him, he panicked, terrified that we would never come back and he wouldn't be able to escape. You had to love that dog to put up with all that.

It wasn't just about understanding what had happened to him in the past, but also about understanding what he needed in life. One day we had a joiner round to do some work. He made a great fuss of Charlie. He trained gun dogs for shooting, so of course he knew how to handle a springer spaniel. He'd only been working a short time when he called me through and said, 'Has your dog got a place where he always hides things? He's a lovely dog, but if I need my hammer I look for it and it's gone. I go into the other room and there's Charlie sitting with it. He's a lovely dog, as I say, but he's stealing everything and now I can't find what he's done with my chisel.'

I led him to Charlie's special hiding place and sure enough, there was the chisel, plus a few other tools that the joiner hadn't even noticed were missing.

'What you need to do,' he told me, 'is get a dog whistle and give that dog some work to do. That's where it's coming from – he's a working dog and he needs to be busy. He's very smart – I could take him out shooting, no problem. I bet he'd know exactly what he was doing.' He got Charlie to sit, which amazed me because I couldn't, and then he made some suggestions. 'When you walk him, you've got to throw him things and get him to retrieve them. When he's home, you can hide treats or toys for him and get him to seek them out. You've got to give him things to do and that'll calm him down.'

That was a real turning point. Once we kept Charlie busy, his bad behaviour began to be transformed into something more playful. Gradually he began to calm down and we started to get a glimpse of the cheeky character with the big heart who was much too clever for his own good – or for ours, sometimes! I think the mad streak was inflicted on him as a puppy by humans. He could be manic, disturbed even, but at heart he was really a gentle character. It was difficult for him to show that, though, because of the way he'd been treated, so instead it was the naughtiness in him that shone through. And in fact he was much more endearing when he was being cheeky and playful than on the rare occasions when he was being as good as gold: he was that naughty schoolboy you can't bring yourself to tell off because he's just so funny and has so much chutzpah.

You had to watch him, though – he was a thief all his life. If you weren't paying attention to him he'd slip up and steal something from you and carry it off, and it was guaranteed to be the thing you needed most – a packet of cigarettes, a shoe, your wallet. Just when you were hunting high and low for it and cursing yourself for losing it, Charlie would reappear with it in his mouth and drop it at your feet with a big grin. It was always undamaged – his teeth never went through a packet of cigarettes or a piece of shoe leather. True, sometimes he'd just hide the things, but that didn't happen so often.

Once I had a friend staying with us and we were about to have a cup of tea in the kitchen when Charlie materialized with one of her expensive Prada shoes in his mouth. He must have got it out of her suitcase. I apologized and told her it was just because he wanted a treat. As I stood up to get him a biscuit, she reprimanded me and said, 'No, that dog's got to learn,' so she shouted at him and Charlie looked bootfaced and dropped it. Then we got on with our tea.

We'd hardly got halfway down the cup when Jim called through, 'Hey! Charlie's running around here with a pair of knickers in his mouth!' and we went out to the hall to see him cantering up and down waving a pair of my friend's knickers over his head. We had a hell of a job to catch him and retrieve them. This time our friend had a sense of humour – she couldn't help laughing. 'That's not a dog,' she said, 'that's a human!'

He liked to sit at the dinner table on his own chair when we had company, keeping an eye on proceedings while we all ate and chatted. He never took anything from our plates, not even on the sly, and when we'd all finished we'd give him a treat. Once somebody offered him a cigarette poking out of the packet and he took it in his mouth as though he was waiting for a light. We were crying with laughter.

Walking him was always a great joy. Springer spaniels are bred to go charging in and out of the undergrowth, flushing up birds. Charlie could do that all day, rampaging through the heather or bracken. He was always excited and loved being taken to new places in the car. He couldn't see water without wanting to be in it and I'd be terrified when he'd fling himself into fast-flowing rivers and swim against the current.

Once the medium Tony Stockwell came to visit and I thought I'd take him up to Loch Lomond with Charlie to see the scenery. Of course, Tony's an immaculate dresser, but he was covered in dog hair before we even pulled up in the car park, and he'd been licked half to death by Charlie, who probably had an inkling about where we were going. We walked along the shore and chucked some stones into the water for Charlie to go plunging in after and then set out along a high pier which jutted way out into the deep water of the loch so that Tony could take a photo of Ben Lomond. Absentmindedly he kicked a stone off the pier and it fell a good 10 feet before it plopped into the loch, but it had barely broken the surface when Charlie took off like a torpedo from behind us and leapt off the pier – *whoosh!* – into clean air. He hit the water with a big splash and started swimming around and snorting, searching for the stone. Poor Tony was mortified – putting my dog in all that danger! But I told him not to worry – Charlie couldn't have been happier. He was just looking for an excuse to get in the water.

It wasn't just our flat that was his territory – it was the Spiritualist church too. Plenty of the congregation could tell you about a day in January 1996 – one of the coldest Januaries ever in Glasgow – when Charlie locked them all out of the church. A service was due to start and the treasurer came round early to show me and Jim where he was going to put some security lights up outside. We left the door of the church open with the keys and our coats inside and followed him out, and we were just remarking how cold it was when I saw Charlie come racing out of the flat and down the corridor towards us and I realized what was going to happen. 'No, Charlie! No!' I yelled, but it was too late – he'd jumped up and slammed the door shut and we were all locked out.

Cars full of worshippers were beginning to arrive and there we were, out in the snow, with Charlie inside barking and barking at us. The medium who was working that night arrived and we had to explain what was going on through our chattering teeth. We peered through the window and there he was, Cheeky Charlie, racing round the church in circles, barking and wagging his tail. Someone called for the president to bring an extra set of keys, but it was half an hour before he could drive over on the black ice and meantime there we all were, stamping our feet and blowing on our hands, calling to Charlie, who was barking away merrily at us all. If only he had been clever enough to open the door!

He and Dronma always had a special friendship and when she talked to him he'd lay his head on hers and listen to every word. He always liked to be the centre of attention and if he was ill or injured, he'd come over all pathetic and hold up a paw and make a funny kind of growly conversation. You could almost talk to him.

'And what's wrong with you, Charlie?'

'Grrumble umble.'

'Och, that's awful. You poor wee dog.'

Such a baby!

When we got our second springer, Meg, when Charlie was about eight, she threw his complicated personality into relief. Meg came to us straight from her mother and she was so sweet as a puppy that her feet barely hit the floor – we all had to pick her up and cuddle her and get our ears licked for our pains. Even now she's fully grown she's never happier than when she's climbing onto your lap. With her big almond-shaped eyes, she looks like Walt Disney's Bambi. As soon as you walk through the door, even if she's never met you before, if she likes you she'll fling herself into your arms.

Charlie, on the other hand, was almost always wary. Like Meg, his animal side was the loving one, and it was the higher part of his consciousness, the more human one, that made him so guarded. Most animals react in the time it takes an impulse to flash to their brain, but you could see Charlie thinking things through and considering the person before him. That gave him a real insight into people who could potentially harm his 'family' and that was why he was so good at being protective. His consciousness was developing right the way through his life, and I think he learned something from us, too.

CHAPTER TWO

A Sixth Sense

When I started work on this book I asked my readers and friends to tell me their stories about animals and spirit, and got an inbox full of e-mails in response. These remarkable tales featured every kind of animal from pot-bellied pigs to parakeets, and people have been kind enough to let me share them with you. It was very hard to pick just a few when they were all so unique, but several themes emerged, and the first that I'm going to talk about is a kind of 'sixth sense' that many of the pets shared. All of these animals had picked up on something long before the people around them had noticed and very often their first instinct was to protect their human loved ones or to be with them. But is this sixth sense natural or supernatural?

This first story is from Kevin Wiggill from Benoni in South Africa:

> *Darren is our middle child. He had a difficult birth and was born with his cord round his neck, which may have led to him having a learning difficulty later on. He was always an*

embattled little boy and when he was really young we realized there was a problem and tried to help as much as possible. He was one of those kids you have to give unconditional love to – you couldn't be cross with him for long. Inevitably when that happens you end up allowing the child a little more freedom than the others.

We own a guest house on a five-acre plot with a host of cats, cows, dogs and geese. I thought we had enough dogs and told the family, 'No more,' but then a friend's bitch had a litter and there was Darren with his big brown eyes, holding up the runt and saying, 'Daddy, can I keep this puppy?' And of course we gave in. That's how we got Bonnie. She was his animal. None of the other children had their own pet like that.

Bonnie was a Staffordshire terrier crossed with a chow and was a really ugly-looking dog, almost like a small hyena. She loved children, but was also an excellent guard dog. We hardly knew if she was around most of the time because she was so quiet, but if there were any potential thieves or opportunistic criminals around, she would start barking and sound the alarm. I knew I could take her warning seriously and would go and investigate, and every time I'd scare off an intruder.

One day I went running when I heard her barking out in the garden. She was snarling away at the herb garden and running in circles round a five-year-old child who belonged to a family staying at our guest house. Something was wrong and Bonnie was clearly trying to keep the boy away from *that patch of the garden, putting her body between him and the herbs and then breaking away to bark ferociously at them.*

I picked up the child and took him to his parents and went back to see what was worrying Bonnie. To my surprise, there was a two-metre long Rinkhals snake – a spitting cobra – concealed among the plants. Had it struck the child it would have easily killed it. Bonnie had protected the child. What made her do that? What force of nature that we cannot see made her take that risk?

It's obvious that Bonnie's acute canine senses helped her spot the hidden snake, but above and beyond that, to me, Bonnie's story is a great example of the naturalness of animals. It wasn't the force of nature working through her, it was even purer than that – the instinct to protect a child that she barely knew was in every fibre of her being. A person might have paused and thought about the possibility of the snake attacking them or mentally run through what could have gone wrong, but an animal is spared that logic and doubt.

Bonnie's totally instinctive response is something that, if we look closely enough at our animals, we can see occurs almost daily in all kinds of ways. You may think that barking is annoying, but it's just your dog looking out for you.

Another everyday talent that a lot of pets share is the ability to know when their owner is returning. A cynic might say they're just looking forward to being fed, but I think there's a little more to it than a love of Whiskas and Pedigree Chum.

Melissa Priddy, from Castle Douglas in Scotland, has owned both a cat and a dog with this uncanny talent:

When I was first dating my husband I had a cat called Mickey who was 15 years old, a big fluffy cat who was more like a dog in personality. I'd had him since I was 12. My husband-to-be and I would walk home and Mickey would come to meet us to escort us back – you'd see this little shadow and then he'd appear. As time went on he started travelling further to greet us and in the end he must have walked a mile to find us and a mile back again. I don't think one night passed without him coming to find us.

Now I have two dogs, a springer called Dillon who's 10, and a black Labrador/springer cross called Shadow, who's three. My job used to involve travelling from Scotland to Birmingham once a month for meetings and on the day I was leaving Dillon would refuse to eat and stay in his bed – unheard of for him! I suppose he picked up signs that I was preparing to go and he knew the routine.

What was more extraordinary was that when I was driving home my husband and children would always phone me when I was about 15 miles away and say, 'You must be nearly home now.' And I'd wonder how on earth they knew. It turned out that the dogs, led by Dillon, would be going crazy with excitement and running to the window to look out. It didn't matter what time I was travelling, they always knew. It became a bit of a game for us!

Looking back, I think Dillon's always had that talent of knowing when I was coming home, because I remember an incident that happened when he was a puppy. Because he wasn't house-trained we had a stair gate like the ones you have when babies are young and need to be kept away from the stairs, and we'd shut him in the kitchen with it while we went out. We came back one day to find Dillon asleep in his basket as if nothing untoward had happened, but then I went into the living room and noticed something missing. 'Where's that big tin of Quality Street chocolates?' I asked my husband. Then I saw them – a trail of empty sweet wrappers round the house and a little heap of the golden penny toffee chocolates. Dillon had raided the tin and eaten all of them apart from his least favourites. Then he'd realized we were coming home and, knowing he'd been naughty, had jumped back over the stair gate to pretend that he was totally innocent!

Dillon is a typical springer spaniel, not just because he knows how to steal sweets but also because these dogs have an amazing sense of time and their owners' comings and goings. Of all the dogs I've owned, Charlie and Meg have had the best sense of when I was on my way home. Charlie would always get excited when a particular friend of his, old Gordon, came round to visit, too. It was handy because that's how we knew to put the kettle on – Gordon didn't let us know when he might pop by!

But how do all these springers and Mickey the cat know when their owners are coming back? Can they smell or hear us coming from miles away with their hyper-alert senses? Scientist Rupert Sheldrake has been studying the sixth sense of animals for decades. He believes that animals (including humans) are connected by 'morphic fields' which enable them to sense or even to see in their mind's eye where they and their loved one or pack members are located, even over huge distances. A school of fish or a flock of birds can know where the other fish or birds are in relation to them and react so that the whole group moves together. They are all individuals, but also part of a bigger unit because of the way they are linked together. They also sense when they're being watched by others who may be a threat, just as Bonnie knew the Rinkhals snake was lurking in the herb garden.

In his book, *Dogs Who Know When Their Owners Are Coming Home*, Sheldrake describes the case of a terrier called Jaytee who had a well-developed ability to sense when his owner, a lady called Pam, was returning from work. The dog stayed with her parents during the day and so they were able to observe his reactions as Pam travelled back to collect him. Dr Sheldrake recorded hundreds of instances when Jaytee would wait at a certain window and watch for Pam. At first Pam's parents would record the little dog's movements and later the scientist set up a camera to follow what Jaytee was up to.

Pam would travel any distance from 4½ to 14 miles away — much too far for the dog to be able to smell her or hear her approach, no matter how good his nose or ears — and then return at a random time. To test Jaytee's ability and be certain that he wasn't associating the sound of a particular vehicle with her, she varied the way she travelled, taking either her own car, another car, a bike, train or taxi. The results were fascinating. Although Jaytee sometimes got distracted or was ill, on most occasions he would gravitate towards the window within 10 minutes of Pam setting off for home. And that was true even when they moved the location of the experiment to Pam's own home or her sister's house.

So how did he know? It couldn't have been a matter of routine or of Jaytee using any of the five ordinary senses. He was clearly relying on something I'd call telepathy, enabled by Sheldrake's morphic fields. It wasn't as if Pam was sitting down and sending out thought waves to her dog either. The whole process was so natural that she was unaware of it.

Many pet owners around the world have sent Sheldrake their accounts of similar phenomena, largely involving dogs but also cats, horses, ferrets, a monkey, parrots and even an owl. It doesn't matter that the two 'senders' are from different species – it's a force that transcends that, like spirit.

In one instance a man was out at the theatre and he got so bored by the play that he started to fantasize about getting up and leaving. At precisely that moment his dog, watched by the man's wife back at home, headed to his usual 'waiting spot'. The man decided to sit through the rest of the play and so came home much later than the dog had anticipated, and the poor pooch probably looked pretty confused! It was his owner's intention to return that he picked up on, not him jingling his keys a few miles away.

Some sceptics would say that these telepathic animals must know that their owners are on their way because they look at the people around them and pick up clues. According to this theory, even if Jaytee didn't know Pam was coming home from work, her parents did and maybe they gave that away with subtle changes of body language that only the terrier could pick up, or maybe Melissa's children got excited because she was on her way back from Birmingham and Dillon noticed. But this story from Ann Shayler of Farnham about her rescue cat Raffles proves there's something else at work:

My ex-husband was a milkman and on his rounds he came across a cat which was only about 10 weeks old and being mistreated. The child in the family that owned her would throw her around and the cat seemed to have something wrong with her back legs as a result of this rough treatment — she walked a bit oddly. My ex-husband rescued her and brought her home.

From the beginning Raffles was a feisty little character. She terrorized the local dog population and she didn't like people — she always stayed a little bit feral, no matter how well we looked after her. If I managed to pick her up, as soon as I put her down she'd try and lick clean everywhere that I'd touched her. The only being on Earth she loved was my son, who was five when we got her, and she shared his childhood. With him she was always very gentle. She'd sleep on his bed and follow him to the park. When he started at school, she'd walk him to the end of the road and then go to meet him in the afternoon when he came home. I assumed she knew when he was coming from the time of day and our body language, and that's why she set out. However, when he grew up and left for university it was a different matter.

After he'd gone, Raffles moved next door to live with an elderly lady. I think she preferred to be there because the lady was quiet and didn't bother her. The funny thing was, whenever my son was coming back from uni to visit, Raffles would reappear in our house and go and lie on his bed to wait for him. She wasn't even living in the house, so she couldn't have picked up any signs from us, and sometimes even we didn't know that my son was going to make a surprise visit. I'll never know how she knew that her favourite person would be back, but there she always was, waiting for him. They really did have an exceptional bond.

Raffles lived to the ripe old age of 21. In the end she was just very tired and weak and when I took her to the vet's (wrapped in a blanket, as she'd never let herself be put in a cat box), she had to be put down. Even though she was so old and so feeble, it took the vet two injections before Raffles drifted away – something he said he'd never seen in all his years of practising.

She was an incredibly strong spirit. I've had 10 cats, but none of them was like Raffles – somehow she was totally different, and even though she was more aloof than any of them, she had so much more character.

This level of communication works through feelings, not language. It also works best when an animal has a strong bond with an individual. Raffles obviously didn't bother nipping round to see Ann or her husband – the cat was only interested in her son! I bet Raffles's strong personality made her especially good at using and understanding those feelings. She was tuned right in to Ann's son, so that he only had to think of coming home and Raffles would know and go to meet him.

Rupert Sheldrake is very sure that these telepathic communications 'depend on bonds between people and animals that are not mere metaphors, but actual connections', and I would agree with him 100 per cent. And of course, being a medium, I would go a step further and say that those bonds of love and affection last beyond death too. They're the same bonds that keep you attached to the spirit of a loved one who has passed if you're open to them and acknowledge them.

Some scientists like to criticize Dr Sheldrake and reject his work out of hand, but now even some of them are beginning to ask questions about animals' intuition and realize that it has important implications for many areas of research. The Chinese have been monitoring animals' behaviour since the 1970s to see if it will alert them to abnormal seismic activity and help save lives in the event of a massive earthquake. In one study in Nanning they keep snakes who are monitored 24 hours a day for warning signs. After the May 2008 earthquake in Sichuan, many Chinese bloggers pointed out that there had been several signs from the natural world: hundreds of toads invading a city, a million butterflies taking flight together and farm animals behaving in a disturbed fashion.

In the medical world, dogs might be able to play their part in the fight against cancer. A study in England by Dr John Church showed that dogs could recognize which patients had bladder cancer by sniffing their urine samples – research that is still ongoing. There are many recorded stories of animals 'worrying' at a mole or patch of skin on their owner, licking it persistently, and the mole later turning out to be cancerous.

One piece of canine intuition that's fascinating biologists but remains essentially a mystery is the ability of some dogs to either alert their owners to the fact that they're about to have an epileptic fit or look after them while the seizure is under way, perhaps by making sure they don't fall onto anything which might injure them. Wendy Bessenyei of Port Elizabeth in South Africa sent me this story about her dog Timone:

I have a five-year-old Jack Russell called Timone, who is my darling. We picked him out for our daughter from a litter of puppies that a friend had bred, although he might have picked us, because I remember him waddling over to investigate us first. We named him Timone after a character in The Lion King, because we already had a cockatiel called Phumba, and the kids were delighted with him. He used to sleep tucked up in a blanket next to my side of the bed, between the mattress and the bedside cupboard till he got too podgy to squeeze in there.

He's a wonderful dog to have around and he likes to come for a drive in the car to the shops and stick his head out of the window and feel the wind in his ears. He calms me down in the evening when I get home from work, as I have a really hectic job as a bank teller. Seeing over 100 people a day can drain you, but just hugging him and having him near me — and, of course, his overbite smile — really melts my heart and makes me smile.

I had a friend to stay who had been having a tough time. She'd been having symptoms of bipolar disorder, which was causing her rapid mood swings and a lot of mental strife. Another doctor had found an 'unknown growth' on the CAT scan of her brain and she'd blacked out at the wheel of her car a few months before and crashed. Although her injuries hadn't been serious, she had understandably been very affected by this and the fact that the doctors didn't seem to be able to diagnose what was wrong with her.

She was sitting side by side with me on the couch in my living room, just chatting to me, when her hands started shaking and she said she felt nauseous. I drew the curtains and put on some soothing Mozart to help her.

Timone was sitting at her feet all this time, watching her and whining softly. He jumped up into her lap, which I thought was odd, because he didn't do that with many people at all, and started licking her hands. She stroked his back and then he climbed up to her shoulder and rested his head against her neck. My friend was increasingly distressed, but she went on stroking Timone. She was getting panicky, so I moved closer and just spoke softly to her, trying to keep her calm and focused. Timone stayed gazing into her face.

Within 10 minutes she'd had a full-blown epileptic fit, which was terrifying for her and for me. I got my husband to take the kids away upstairs and sat with her as she rode it out. I felt so helpless that I just rubbed her shoulder and held her hand. It lasted a few minutes, maybe five or 10, but it seemed longer. I spoke calmly to her when it seemed to have finished and told her to take deep breaths. Timone had stayed on her lap throughout and now he jumped down, yawned and lay down at our feet again.

My friend was crying and kept saying she was sorry, but I soothed her and helped her put her pyjamas on and climb upstairs to bed. I was amazed at the way that Timone had sensed what was going to happen and instinctively acted to comfort her. She had never had an attack before and hadn't known what was happening, and as far as I know Timone had never come across anyone with epilepsy.

Much later my friend told me that she'd had other fits since then and usually they'd left her muscles sore and her whole body exhausted, but that something about having Timone to stroke helped her both before and after that particular episode. It just elevates my respect for dogs to a new level. Their spiritual ways are far superior to our warmongering, materialistic focus on this earthly plane.

It's thought that dogs like Timone smell tiny changes in body chemistry or pick up on a difference in the electrical currents in the epileptic's brain. It's not so much a sixth sense that helps them pick up these clues as being more in tune with the five 'normal' senses we share with them – sight, smell, sound, touch and taste – than most of us ever are.

Some organizations now train 'support dogs' to look after their owners and to get help when they have an attack. Humans witnessing another person having a seizure often react with fear – something you might expect a dumb animal to do too, but although these dogs alert their owners by showing agitation, they also stick to their side and often lick them back to consciousness. It's impossible to train a dog to 'sense' that their owner is about to become ill before it happens, though; that's something dogs – both the common-or-garden pets and the specially trained support dogs – learn for themselves through their own bond with their owner.

This bond is crucial for support dogs. The would-be owners must attend several days of training during which they complete tasks with lots of different dogs and eventually either choose the pup they're drawn to or the pup chooses them. Many epileptics report that after a few months with their new companion and helpmate, they start to have fewer fits – probably because they are less stressed now that they know when they are about to have an attack and feel they will be safe when it happens.

I think what's really interesting about Timone's tale is that he wasn't bonded with this lady – this little dog just had such a big heart that it didn't matter that she was a stranger to him. He certainly hadn't had any training, but he was there to help ground the woman when she needed it most. Timone knew he needed to be still and comfort her while her world was turning upside down.

When strong feelings like this are involved, there can be another layer to the 'sixth sense': time. Telepathy works outside time because it's a feeling thing, a phenomenon that's powered by pure emotion, so sometimes telepathic messages can be about something that hasn't happened yet but will.

Premonitions are not something you can sit down and decide to have because you want to. You often have to be in a really extreme situation that pushes you 'out of time' and into more expanded consciousness. People who are grief-stricken or terrified are more likely to experience one and although it will seem 'paranormal' and 'illogical' to them, they'll know instinctively that it's real.

For an animal it's different. They don't need that extreme emotion because they're already living in a way that's much more in tune with their feelings. They won't apply logic or talk themselves out of it, just respond.

Of course, you can't exactly ask your cat to tell you next week's winning lottery number, but sometimes a pet has an unmistakable reaction and future events will explain it.

In *The Unbelievable Truth* I told an uncanny story about one of the many occasions when Charlie seemed to be sensing something beyond everyday human perception. When Jim and I were out walking with him in a local cemetery he found a granite headstone with the words 'Gordon Smith, writer' carved on it, and under that, 'Steven Andrew Smith', an able seaman who had died at sea during World War One. As my own son was called Steven Andrew Smith and he had joined the Royal Navy only a week before, I was chilled to the marrow, especially as Charlie was barking at the stone as if he was terrified.

A little over a month later, my son left the navy, having decided it wasn't the life for him. When the second Gulf War kicked off a short time later, I wondered whether in some alternative future my own Steven Andrew Smith had been killed in action and Jim and I had been standing at his graveside.

Much later Jim and I went back to the cemetery to look at the gravestone once more and did a double-take when we saw that there wasn't a trace of the young man's name. 'Gordon Smith, writer' was still engraved on the stone, as was the name of a daughter who'd died in the 1920s, but Steven Andrew Smith had vanished. This time it was Meg who led us to the spot and she showed no interest or fear whatsoever.

What had Charlie known when he'd found the headstone? Had he been scared because he had picked up the ominous meaning of those names on the granite? I'll never know what it meant to Charlie, but I know that he was trying to warn us about something that was going to happen in the future. Jim and I would never have found that inscription in a cemetery full of thousands, and besides, we weren't looking for it – why should we?

Anita Robertson of Keighley in England told me about another dog who predicted the future:

> My friend's mum Ann once told me a story involving her dog, a golden Labrador. One Sunday in the wintertime her in-laws came round for dinner as usual and that day, oddly, the dog wouldn't leave Ann's mother-in-law alone. As she sat at the table eating her food the dog put its head in her lap and when she moved to the sofa it sat by her feet, whimpering. In the end they had to put it in the garden.
>
> Later that evening, after the in-laws had gone home, Ann opened the front door to put the milk bottles out and the Labrador rushed past her and ran away. This dog was so pampered it had fresh mince every day and lots of love and attention, so this made no sense. Ann was distraught. She quickly put her shoes on and called her husband, Roy, and they set out to try and find the dog on the dark streets. They lived in an area with many busy roads and the dog was never left to wander but was always taken out on a lead, so they were very concerned about its welfare.
>
> Anyway, they came back empty-handed, hoping the dog would be on the doorstep waiting for them, but it wasn't. The phone rang and it was Ann's mother-in-law, saying, 'Ann, you won't believe it, but your dog is here and it will not let me alone.' By this time it was about 10 p.m., so they decided to leave the dog there and go and pick it up the next day.
>
> A few hours later Ann and Roy got a phone call from Roy's father. Ann's mother-in-law had collapsed and died just after

talking to them – no warning, no illness, just gone. The doctor explained that she'd had a cerebral aneurysm. Ann said she believed the dog had known her mother-in-law was going to die and had gone to comfort her.

This Labrador reminds me of Oscar, the cat who visits the dying in the nursing home, but there's a really important difference. Some biologists have speculated that Oscar knows he has to comfort the elderly patients because he can pick up the physical signs of the fact that they are going to pass, but Ann's mother-in-law died unexpectedly and from something that wouldn't have had any outward physical symptoms.

Animals are linked to death in a subtler way than humans are. They know when a fellow animal is going to die and whether they should be comforted or left alone. They also frequently know when they themselves are going to die and it's very common for cats, for example, to take themselves quietly off when their time has come.

This Labrador had sensed the life force leaving the old lady – there was nothing remarkable or 'psychic' about it, any more than there is about a human 'sensitive' picking up the same clues. It's a natural thing – for us as well as the animals. The difference is that they experience this sixth sense with absolute clarity and they don't cloud their mind with worries about whether it's real or not. We might sit around and say, 'I feel bad about your mother, I don't know what it is,' but we're not going to sit in her lap, lick her hand or follow her home! We'll try and argue ourselves out of the emotion instead, thinking, 'I'm just being daft, she'll be fine!' Paying attention to our own sixth sense is something we can learn from animals.

CHAPTER THREE

~

Animal Compassion

When I was married to Katie, and Steven and Paul were little, we lived in a tenement house in Glasgow and I worked at the barber's. On the top floor of our building there was a young mother with two kids. She was in a bad way – she was an alcoholic who barely seemed to be holding it together. One thing that family did have was a big black lurcher who was an extraordinarily smart and compassionate dog. Every afternoon at the same time the dog would leave the flat and trot down the stairs, and it wouldn't be distracted if you tried to give it a pat on the head or fuss it. At 2:50 p.m. it'd always break into a run and disappear out of the street. At 3:15 p.m. it would reappear at the end of the street with those two little kids, one on either side, each with a hand on its back. The dog would walk slowly enough for their little legs to keep up and they would chat away to it, telling it what they'd done at school all day. It would take them right back into the building and up to the flat to their mother.

Everybody in the street knew about that dog and the way it saw those kids home safely. I used to wonder how it started to do that. Maybe the mother used to walk it to the school and as time went on and she got more ill, she left the dog to it. It knew the right time too.

Now that dog didn't have to care, but it did. It could have run away and found a better owner, or struck out on its own and left the responsibility of caring for those children behind, but I don't think that occurred to it. Those kids and their mother were its pack and it did its best by them.

Years later I was reminded of that lurcher's compassion when I was listening to a wonderful man called Bill Jordan speaking at the London Spiritual Mission's annual pets' service. Bill is a vet who's been awarded an OBE for dedicating much of his life to working for the RSPCA and international wildlife organizations. He's travelled the world widely and reported back on the welfare of animals to help in campaigns against bullfighting, seal clubbing and fur trapping, and he knows more than a little about compassion himself. He and my friend Roz organized the annual animal service in Notting Hill to raise money for charities local and international and to educate people about animal welfare. Everyone would bring their pets along – dogs, cats, guinea pigs, birds in cages, even a boa constrictor once – and the pets would all settle quietly for the service. There was a wonderful ambience that meant that they didn't fret or fight each other but remained peaceful. The service was incredibly popular and grew every year. This is one of the stories I remember Bill telling us.

Once when he was on one of his fact-finding trips overseas, Bill was watching an elephant that was being used to help lay the foundations of a new building. At a command from its handler, it would pick up an enormous wooden column in its trunk, turn it upright and lower it carefully into a hole.

Everything was proceeding smoothly when suddenly the great beast stopped what it was doing. The handler hit it and shouted, but it wouldn't budge. It held the tree trunk firmly and wouldn't drop it. Everyone began swearing and yelling at it and tugging it this way and that, but it wouldn't shift a foot.

Eventually someone went to look in the next hole to see if there was anything there that had frightened the elephant. There, several feet down at the very bottom, was a kitten that had obviously fallen in. If the elephant had dropped the tree trunk into the hole, the cat would have been crushed. The workers removed the kitten before the elephant's eyes and then work resumed and the elephant once more did their bidding without a fuss.

Now tell me, why should that elephant have cared about the kitten? It's not as though a kitten would be food for an elephant or that it could help it out or do anything useful for it. And there was no way that Nellie could have mistaken a cat for a fellow elephant. What Bill witnessed was a very animal kind of empathy, one that enabled that elephant to have a complete connection to that cat and to fear injuring it. Once it had realized what was going on, it saw no alternative but to protect the kitten.

Lots of mediums I know have pets who seem happy to get involved in their work. Dogs and cats can give excellent counselling, even if they don't have the certificates for it. I don't push my dogs out of the room when someone comes for a reading, unless that person really can't handle pets or has an allergy.

Once I was giving a reading at home to an actress who'd turned up in a beautiful black outfit and I warned her to fend Meg off or she'd be covered in white hair, but she told me not to worry because she loved dogs. As we went on with the reading she got very teary and emotional, and I realized with embarrassment that we didn't have any proper hankies in the house and I'd have to offer this glamorous lady a piece of loo roll to mop up her tears! That's when Meg did something she'd never done in a reading before: she hopped onto the woman's lap and licked off her tears. I told my sitter just to push her away, but she insisted, 'No, just leave her – that's the sweetest thing for her to do!'

Even though she is very much a dog's dog, Meg is the most loving pet I have ever owned. Her sense of affection towards people is growing day by day and it's beautiful to watch. Don't be fooled by this touching story, though – she's still as mad as a box of frogs.

Charlie knew his role at a reading too, even before the sitter had walked up the drive. Normally he barked if strangers were approaching the house, but when someone was coming for a reading he wouldn't stir, not even when they rang the doorbell. He had his special little ritual: he'd accompany us from the door to the chair and then when they sat down he'd rest his head on their knee and look them in the eye. I would reassure the sitter that he did that for everyone and that he'd settle soon, and sure enough he'd sit or lie at the person's feet as if to be a comforting presence and he'd stay there until the reading was over. Nothing could perturb him.

There's one reading that I can't forget and I don't think the sitter will ever forget either. When she arrived, she looked as though she was just about holding herself together, but once we'd got her installed in the armchair her lip quivered and she started to cry and cry. Jim tried to give her a hug and offer her a cup of tea or a glass of water, but she just cried harder. She couldn't get a word out for sobs. They went right up through her body, racking her from head to toe. I tried to reassure her and help her relax while Jim ran for tissues, but it was no use – she just couldn't stop herself. Jim and I were out in the corridor hissing to each other, 'What can we do? She can't stop!' and then scuttling back in to try and pat her back; and then Charlie settled the matter. He'd been sitting at her feet, keeping an eye on things, and then he got up and, well, there's no delicate way of putting this, started humping the lady's leg. We were horrified and rushed to pull him off, but the lady looked down at Charlie busily working away and her sobs turned to laughter – laughter as strong as the sobs had been. Charlie immediately dismounted, turned to me and Jim as if to say, 'You see? That's all it needed,' and left the room as if nothing had happened. Then we cracked up too. The three of us laughed till we had tears streaming down our faces and our stomachs hurt. Trust Cheeky Charlie!

My friend the medium Billy Cook used to be accompanied everywhere by his great friend Tilbury, a wee black, white and grey Lhasa Apsu/Jack Russell cross. Tilbury had been the runt of the litter, but he had a big personality to make up for it and he turned out to be a priceless friend to Billy. He travelled up and down the country with him as he visited Spiritualist churches and he liked to sit in on the services. If the congregation were good singers, Tilbury would howl along with them, and if he didn't like their musical efforts, he'd just sit and bark at them! He also used to start barking at the exact time Billy was supposed to wrap up what he was doing – which was really useful because Billy never knew when to stop!

When it came to private readings, Tilbury was even more intuitive. He always knew whether the person who walked in the door was really grieving or just there out of curiosity and taking up an appointment that could have truly helped someone else. If they were just there to gawp, he would take one look at them and stalk off. If he sensed that they were devastated and wrestling to keep themselves together, though, he'd leap up onto their lap and lick them.

Billy always talks about one particular sitter Tilbury really helped with. A young girl had turned up at Billy's door and she looked so haggard and ill that Billy thought she was probably a junkie. Drug addicts have great problems and issues, but it's difficult for a medium to help them when they're already in another world. So Billy was feeling very sceptical about this girl, but Tilbury didn't hesitate. He clung to her and followed her from room to room, finally climbing onto her lap when she sat down. So Billy gave her the benefit of the doubt and as the reading began he realized that the little dog had been spot on. The girl wasn't a junkie, but the loss of a loved one had driven her to anorexia. Even with his medium's intuition, Billy hadn't been able to work her out, but Tilbury had reached out to her and made sure his owner helped her. That was a dog who had true spiritual abilities.

Dogs are often called man's best friend, but cats have a reputation for being selfish and aloof. Kevin Wiggill in South Africa is blessed not only with Bonnie the dog but also a cat called Garfield, who showed how silly that assumption was when he proved an excellent nurse to Kevin's wife. Kevin explains:

One Boxing Day, which was also my son Darren's birthday, in comes Darren with a tiny black kitten, its eyes hardly open, saying, 'Look what I've been given for my birthday.' Someone had left the little cat on the lawn and Darren was the one who found her. So that was that, you couldn't tell him he couldn't have a cat. He called her Garfield.

Garfield had an extraordinary sense of compassion. When my wife Julie was suffering from ovarian cancer and having a torrid time with chemo, she was her constant companion, lying on her bed most of the day. I don't agree with animals on the furniture and especially not with cats on the bed at night, but Julie was so frail she was almost bedridden and the cat was a comfort to her.

When she wanted to go to the toilet she would ring a bell and wherever we were in the house we would hear it and go to help her. Our house is quite large and the distance from Julie's room to the guest dining room where the family was sitting one evening watching TV was probably about 25 metres. This was about a week before Julie passed.

We were all settled in when suddenly Garfield came racing into the room, screaming as though she'd been burned with a red-hot poker. Of course we all jumped up to see what was wrong with her but she would not let us catch her and kept heading back towards Julie's bedroom, still screaming as she went. She kept this up till we reached Julie, then stopped. Only then did we realize that Julie was not in bed – she had fallen out and was lying on the floor in pain, but she was so ill that she could not reach the bell or shout for help. Garfield had known what to do. And they say animals can't talk.

I think the stories of Garfield, Tilbury and Bill's elephant show us that compassion is present in all forms of life.

Animals can't read your thoughts, but they pick up on your feelings, and they're wonderful at that. We aren't so good at it now because we try to communicate at one remove with words. We say, 'Yeah, I feel OK,' when our gut is telling us we're feeling terrible, and the person we're talking to thinks, 'They don't look good, but they say they're OK, so I'll leave it. Besides, they might think I'm interfering.' Animals just know that you're low, and their innocence means they'll go straight to you to offer comfort. It doesn't occur to them to hold back in case you don't want the attention – they don't even think about it. That's their purity. They can't pretend, and when they receive our feelings they have to act.

When I was working in South Africa in April 2008 I heard Philippa Johnson's story about her experiences with a horse who helped her when her life was changed almost beyond recognition:

I have ridden and worked with horses my whole life and as a child I was lucky enough to have my own pony, but unfortunately my family couldn't afford a horse for me. This wasn't a problem, as my uncle owned a large competitive stables and there were always horses that needed to be worked, so I was able to build my skills as a horsewoman and hoped one day to compete in dressage at the highest level.

When I turned 21, my mum and dad said they'd help me buy a horse, and my brother, Brett, found an interesting ad in one of the trading magazines for a young warmblood. I phoned the number and the woman who was selling the horse said it would be no problem for us to come over and take a look. She added that she liked to keep her horses 'light' as too much protein was bad for their joints.

Dad and I drove out and upon arriving were shown into a dark smelly cowshed. There was an enormous two-and-a-half-year-old warmblood there. You could see almost every bone in his body and he was so thin that it looked as though his hipbones might come through his skin at any moment. We took him outside.

He had only just been introduced to a saddle, so we started slowly with me lying across the saddle before putting my full weight on it. I walked and trotted him round a small clearing in the veld, but I couldn't do any more because of lack of education on his part and also lack of space.

On the way back Dad said, 'That horse has the three things you look for in a dressage horse: rhythm, temperament and cadence.' I thought either he was crazy or he had too much faith in my ability if he thought I could make that poor thing into a dressage champion. We talked more and Dad pointed out that even if I only kept him for a year and it didn't work out, the lessons I'd put in would increase his value and I could use the money for another horse. We decided to send the vet to check the young warmblood.

The vet phoned that evening and told us that the horse would have been dead by that evening as he was so sick with biliary. The woman who owned him hadn't noticed there was anything wrong! We brought him back to the yard for treatment, but when Dad and my uncle went to collect him they had to link hands behind his quarters and almost lift him into the trailer because he was so weak.

He stayed at my uncle's until he was fully recovered and we decided to buy him outright from his owner. We had left him a stallion so that the extra testosterone would help him pull through and once he was well he was still so good-natured that we didn't change that. His name was Sundowner Kingpin, aka Boyzie, as he was my baby boy.

At the end of October 1998 I was involved in a car accident in which I lost my brother and my boyfriend. I was severely injured down my right side and was unconscious for some time. My dressage coach made sure that the first thing I saw when I opened my eyes was a photo of Boyzie.

I had lost all movement down my right-hand side and the doctors told me I would never ride again, as I wouldn't be able to use my right arm. They weren't sure if my right leg would recover or not. Luckily I started to get some use back in my right leg and one night in hospital I made two promises to my best friend. I told her I would walk by the end of the following week (at that stage they still hadn't managed to get me to sit up without throwing up and passing out), and that come 1 January 1999 I would be back in the saddle.

I walked my first length of the parallel bars in the physiotherapy clinic on the Wednesday, and on 1 January, with a lot of help, I got back on Boyzie, who by this stage was a huge 17.3hh stallion. Dad slowly led me round the arena twice and I knew the doctors were wrong. I would ride again.

Before I could start riding properly I needed a nerve graft, which meant I had to put my plans on hold for a few months, but when I did start Boyzie was phenomenal. Every time I lost my balance and tipped forward (I still had no muscles on my right side) he would stop and wait for me to recover and then gently move on. Our progress was incredibly frustrating. Before the accident I had been a young professional who was about to go to Germany to train with some of the best in the business and now it was hard for me even to sit straight on my horse.

Boyzie absorbed all my anger, misery and frustration but never let it affect him. A year after my accident we entered our first show. I'd had to downgrade us both all the way to novice level as I was so limited in the movements I could make, but we won, and of course we both wanted more. I entered another show which was in about three weeks.

The day before the show I was about to start exercising Boyzie and my coach asked if I needed any help, but of course by then I thought I could do everything and tried to mount Boyzie without her holding his head. He took two tiny steps forward and it was enough for me to lose my balance and fall awkwardly back into the wall of the indoor arena. I don't know who was more surprised, me or Boyzie – in all the years I'd had him I'd never fallen off him – but I was very seriously injured and couldn't move. My coach tried to stay calm and to get to me to help, but every time she came near me Boyzie would push her away. Finally she had to lead him back to his stable and then get help.

I had broken my back and was not allowed to ride for another six months. Coming so soon after my car accident, this was devastating news, but I decided that as there was nothing I could do about it, I should do what I could instead. Just because I couldn't ride Boyzie didn't mean I couldn't work with him. I wanted to do something called 'joining up'. This is a technique pioneered by the original horse whisperer, Monty Roberts. It involves setting the horse loose and then using body language to reach a point where the horse chooses to come back to you and to work with you, giving you its full trust.

Lisa, the occupational therapist who was helping me, did join-ups with the horses and ponies she used for therapeutic riding, so I asked her to help. We took Boyzie to the indoor arena and let him go, and then Lisa successfully did a join-up with him. When it was my turn, everything went perfectly until the last moment. Just as he was about to walk towards me, Boyzie suddenly tossed his head and cantered off. This happened several times.

Finally Lisa said, 'There's something going on between the two of you and you need to resolve it first. He wants to join up, but there's something stopping him.'

At that stage I was working with a fantastic healer called Steve who used muscle testing to find out what might be troubling me or holding back my recovery. I asked him if he'd be willing to try with Boyzie and he agreed, although he'd never worked with animals before.

We went to the stables together and the first thing he did was to ask Boyzie if I could be his surrogate, and Boyzie agreed. I stood with my right shoulder against his shoulder and used my left arm for the testing. We checked if there was anything physically wrong first, but there were no problems there.

By this stage Boyzie was standing in the middle of the box, head down and chewing – a sign that he was relaxed and trusting us. Steve then told me that as he started testing again I must visualize my fall. The very nanosecond I started to picture the fall in my mind's eye, Boyzie's head shot up and he raced to the back of the stable, rolling his eyes and snorting.

Steve was quick to understand. 'There's the problem – he doesn't want to join up with you because by making you his leader, he, as the stallion, can't protect you.' In the wild the stallion's job is to protect his herd and that's just what Boyzie was doing with me.

After my accident Boyzie and I had many difficult times, but his loyalty never failed. I may have saved him when he was young, but he saved me too, and for that I can never repay him.

Philippa went on to win not one but two silver medals at the 2004 Paralympics.

I think that Boyzie is very evolved; he displays two of the highest spiritual virtues, wisdom and compassion. Not many humans display both.

If we look closely at our animals, it won't take us too long to see that there are all levels of these star qualities in them, just as there are in humans. In the same way that we witness people who have shown amazing compassion in their lives, whether through a vocation like nursing or when some harm came to those around them, we can see animals that are truly exceptional. Patch, who was looked after by Terry Davies of Llanelli in Wales, was one of them:

Patch was a mongrel dog who was in our family for 16 years. He was always there for me when I needed him and fitted happily into our household of three cats and later another dog, Tia.

My mother lived opposite us in a terraced house and her friend, a neighbour of ours, was a lovely lady called Rose, who lived alone and loved animals. She was just one of four OAPs that Patch would sneak off and pay social calls to; no matter what we did to keep him in he'd find a way and off he'd go. We worried about the risks he took with crossing the road, but there was no stopping him keeping his appointments! He kept up his daily routine for the last six years of his life and was a blessing to the four elderly people. He really lifted their spirits and they drew great comfort from him.

On two occasions, however, he didn't shift from his basket. Later we got phone calls or visits from some of his friends to ask if he was safe and well, and nothing seemed wrong with him. It turned out, though, that those were the days when my mum and Rose sadly passed. Patch obviously knew before we did.

When he himself got old he would still make the effort to go on his rounds, although he didn't always make it, but his pensioner friends would call us every day to check how he was. It was a testament to his loyalty. The good he generated in his life for these people was priceless, as they were in real need of company. Our lesson from Patch was to look more deeply at how we conducted ourselves with friends.

Now, not every dog is like Patch, but then again, not every human is like Mother Teresa! We all have the capacity to go beyond what's expected of us in life, though, and that's just what Patch did. A cynic would say he was just after an extra biscuit or two, but I doubt it. If it had just been a Pavlovian reaction to jammy dodgers, he would have carried on looking for his treats after his friends had passed. That dog was just giving his services, like any person who volunteers to visit the residents in an old folks' home or mentor young kids in their spare time. He was something special, the kind of dog that the Tibetans would say had a consciousness that would give it a higher rebirth in its next life. He was a pure giver of love and a compassionate being and, as Terry says, if a dog can do that, we have to think about what we humans have to offer.

CHAPTER FOUR

~

Bonds between Animals

A friend once told me an unforgettable story. She ran a riding stables with a large number of horses, one of which was a very elderly Shetland pony. The pony went lame and so they called in the vet, who said that he was sorry, but the old pony had broken his leg and there was nothing he could do. It was probably best to put him down.

My friend and the grooms all said goodbye to the pony and made a fuss of him, then stood back as someone led him out of his stable. They wanted to walk him a little distance away and behind a barn so that the other horses wouldn't see his end and be distressed, but this is when an extraordinary thing happened.

When they heard their old companion being walked away, the other horses all came to the front of their boxes and began to stamp on the floor and strike at the doors of their stables, as though they were marking a march. They wouldn't look at any of the people, just flung their heads up in the air. All round the yard this deafening drumming built up, getting louder as the pony disappeared out of sight. At the exact moment that he was euthanized, the horses all let out an uncanny scream. My friend said it was more highly pitched than any sound she'd ever heard them make before, almost like a cry of horror. She never heard them do it before or afterwards. They'd definitely known that the pony was going to die. Was this their way of giving him courage when they sensed he was afraid? Or were they mourning? And why should those horses care if the old pony passed?

In most of my work as a medium I'm working with humans, and animals tend to appear only in connection to people they've loved in life. Of course I can never bring a message through *for* an animal, although the first time I led the animal service at the London Spiritual Mission I thought I'd have some fun. Everyone was very quiet, so after I'd introduced myself and said I was going to tune in to spirit, I pretended I had a connection and began nodding. Then I went to a black Labrador in the front row, and said, 'Now I've never had this happen before. I've got a message from your mother. She's says you've six sisters and you all look very alike.' And the dog cocked its head and looked at me, and nobody said a word. Everyone was so serious, I had to tell them I was just kidding! Maybe I should have pretended to go into a trance and started barking!

Just because a medium can't pass a message from a spirit animal to an animal on this plane doesn't mean those animals can't communicate with each other. We've already seen how animals have the ability to communicate telepathically with each other and to sense the pain or joy of others. Here are two stories where an exceptional bond between two pets lasted beyond the grave. Roy McKeag from Beith in Ayrshire, Scotland, goes first.

I used to have two border collies called Bess and Sonny. Bess was the mother and Sonny her boy (Son of Bess!) They were the most intelligent and amazing dogs. They went everywhere with me and if they couldn't go, then I couldn't go either. People always mentioned how well behaved they were and what great personalities they had.

In the evening the dogs and I would usually sit in the lounge. Bess would lie on a rug in front of the radiator below the window and I would sit in an armchair at the opposite side of the room next to the fire. Sonny would always lie at my feet.

Bess died very suddenly from liver and kidney failure and Sonny and I were devastated. I had never seen an animal react in such a way to the death of another animal. Sonny ran about the garden howling – something he'd never done in his life before. He was grieving badly. He became a very quiet dog in the immediate aftermath of Bess's passing.

A few weeks later I was sitting in front of the log fire with Sonny at my feet when he suddenly shot up and looked over at the door. He looked at me again and then back at the door. He repeated this a few times and I felt he was confused. I also sensed that Bess was standing there.

Sonny then slowly turned his gaze across the room towards the radiator as if he was watching Bess walking across the room as she used to. He stopped moving his head when he was looking directly at the radiator. He kept staring at the radiator, then turning to me, then looking back at it again; he had an expression of bewilderment. Then he slowly got up and walked over to the radiator and had a good sniff about. He returned to my feet, but gazed at the radiator for the rest of the evening. This happened several more times over the next few weeks.

Slowly Sonny returned to his normal self and the number of times he watched 'Bess' make her way to her old spot decreased. But Bess had let us know that her spirit was still with us and I'm sure Sonny could see it on those occasions.

Sonny has now passed too, but I am often aware of the presence of both him and his mother when I'm out on the hills where they loved to chase about, or sitting quietly by a log fire on a winter's night.

Of course animals see the pain and grief of other animals when they are hurt or sick or when they go into the spirit world, and like many people they still feel the presence of their loved ones after death. Unlike many of us, though, animals recognize this for what it is and react to it and then they get on with their lives. Recognition, reaction and acceptance are all key to such episodes and to overcoming grief. It's not as though Sonny went around afterwards saying, 'Oh, my God!' He just let it be. And I'm sure he took comfort from knowing that his mother was still in her spot.

The second story also comes from my part of the world. I met Dawn Murray up in Perthshire for the filming of a documentary about bereavement at a pet cemetery out in the open countryside on a glorious day, with two red kites wheeling overhead. I was intrigued by her job as a pet undertaker and immediately impressed by her warmth and compassion.

At her home in the Borders, Dawn arranges dignified send-offs for pets on behalf of their owners, many of whom have found themselves faced with the stark reality of having to see an animal that's been a member of their family tossed into an anonymous incinerator. She also uses her professional training as a counsellor to comfort people and offers to be present when an animal is put down, should the owners need her support at the time. So many people feel sheepish or wrong for mourning a pet and just the fact that Dawn's there to tell them it's OK to feel as though their hearts have been broken is a great relief to them.

Now in this story there are some bad guys who happen to be animals – a pair of Staffordshire bull terriers. You might say that the way they behave makes a nonsense of everything I've said about animals being spiritual beings and having higher souls, but of course that's the wrong conclusion to take away. Just as not every person can be Mother Teresa, not every dog can be Patch. Maybe, like their human equivalent, some learn to act and to think with the lowest parts of their consciousness. The cat that plays with a mouse or the killer whale that tortures a sea lion is on the same level of consciousness as the human who abuses another human or animal. Humans stalk, chase, torture and kill too. We do it because we can and it shows our superiority, and maybe the cat or the Staffies in this story have the same reasons. It's not human nature, it's nature full stop, and within it there's cruelty. Humans and animals that do develop their consciousness can lift themselves out of this cycle, because if you're highly evolved you cannot harm another animal or being – you know that you will only harm yourself. Perhaps that's a lesson for another book!

Here's Dawn's tale, which is all about an exceptional friendship between two animals.

When I got my white greyhound Kaz he was already quite old. He'd had a working life as a racing dog and after that his trainer had handed him over to the Glasgow Veterinary College, where he served for six years as a blood donor. Greyhound blood is exceptionally good, with a high red blood cell count, so vets prefer to use it for transfusions. The dogs are also very docile, so don't need to be sedated when they donate, and they're big, so they can give a large quantity of blood. Kaz was well loved by everyone at the college and extremely well looked after, but after five or six years he was too old to carry on giving blood and was put up for rehoming.

I adopted him in 2001, when I'd just finished my job as a senior purser for P&O. I lived on an estate on the south side of Glasgow and Kaz and I would go out for a gentle walk several times each day. Greyhounds are very fit but have no stamina, so our walks were only 15 minutes long, but we went early in the morning, at lunch, at teatime and later on at night.

We were always joined along the way by one or two of the local cats, called Smokey and Tigger, who didn't seem to be scared of the big white dog. One spring I noticed a little black-and-white cat sitting outside one of the houses. He was always crying and I wondered why the people in the house didn't take him in – he seemed to be just a kitten and that crying would have driven me nuts!

The local kids told me his name was Denzil and it took him about a week to get up the nerve to join us. Now we would set out with me and Kaz first and then the three cats following on like a wee train of elephants. The estate had been built with families in mind and there were a lot of green areas and bits of shrubbery. We'd walk round there with the cats and as we walked back the cats would peel off one by one and return to their houses.

I tried giving Denzil some biscuits to see if it would stop him crying and after that he was always there for the walks and the food. I learned a little bit about him from other people on the estate, who said that his original owner had got him as a kitten nine years previously and he'd lived in the house where I'd originally seen him. He'd been brought up with a white greyhound, so I suppose he felt at home with Kaz. After that he'd adopted another family, who'd then moved on and left him behind, but his original owners hadn't been interested in taking him back because they thought he'd just find another home of his own accord. That's why he'd been crying outside their house. He wasn't interested in stepping off his territory and coming to my house, though, and I just saw him as another friend for Kaz to walk with.

I had three years with Kaz, who was a beautiful, lovely dog. Normally the latest I walked him was 9 p.m., but when my mother died my whole pattern was knocked out of order and one night shortly afterwards I didn't get him out till 11 p.m. He was on the lead and we went out to the usual bit of grass, unaccompanied by the cats for once because it was so late. Then a young man with two Staffordshire terriers came round the corner. The dogs weren't on the lead and I later found out that the man had been training them as fighting dogs.

They leapt on poor Kaz, two against one, and began mauling him. He didn't stand a chance. I tried desperately to save him and kicked one of the Staffies off, but it was too late. I got Kaz to the vet immediately, but he was an old dog and the puncture wounds were so severe that even after he'd been patched up by the vet he started to have fits. He was virtually paralysed and when I got him back home I had to wrap him up in his coat and use it as a kind of support to help him outside, holding his hind legs off the ground. There were no more walks; he couldn't move more than a stone's throw from the house.

One day when I was helping him walk a little way away from the house, Denzil appeared and came galloping up to us as fast as he could. He meowed at Kaz and rubbed himself under his belly. They gave each other a wee kiss and then Denzil just stood and watched as I tried to half carry, half support Kaz.

I took the dog to the vet a few weeks later and he was pleased with him, but warned me that when he went downhill it would be very rapid. I got enough medication to last him over Christmas and the New Year and control his fits, but he never made it that far. By the following Wednesday he was deteriorating so badly that he couldn't walk or get up to pee and he'd had a stroke. It was absolutely heartbreaking.

I sat up with him that night and at midnight I heard crying. I thought it was a baby at first, but I couldn't see anyone when I peered out of the window. Eventually I realized that it was coming from the back of the house and I opened the door to find Denzil on the doorstep. I was surprised because he'd never been near our house, as far as I knew. I let him in and he sat by Kaz all night, watching him.

Early the next morning I picked him up gently and put him down outside, saying, 'On you go. See you around, pal.' I shut the door and, with a heavy heart, called the vet. A few hours later he arrived to put Kaz to sleep and I said goodbye to my beautiful dog and friend.

I phoned a pet crematorium and a young lad came round to take Kaz away. I warned him that the dog would be heavier than he looked, but he just hefted him up so violently that he staggered and Kaz's neck broke. I was too stunned to say anything, but followed the lad out to the van with Kaz's favourite toy, which I wanted cremated with him, and I don't think the boy realized I was watching because he just slung Kaz's body into the back of the van. It's because of the way that he was treated then that I ended up deciding to become a pet undertaker.

I went out for the rest of the day and came home later to find Denzil on my doorstep. I let him in and he went racing round the house from room to room, as fast as he could, and when he couldn't find Kaz he shot out of the front door. He did this for 10 straight days in a row. I couldn't believe it, but supposed he'd understand in the end. I'd just leave the door open after he came in so he could get back out again immediately.

At the end of the 10 days I got Kaz's ashes back from the crematorium in an urn. I didn't know what to do with them, so I put them up on a high chest of drawers in my bedroom. This was Christmas Eve. Once more, there was Denzil on the doorstep. I opened the door and in he ran, went straight to my bedroom and gave a blood-curdling scream. I raced in and there he was, back arched, tail fluffed up twice its size. He spun round and charged out of the door. I was thinking, 'Did I really see that happen? Did something else frighten him?' It seemed too much of a coincidence.

A few hours later I heard him crying outside the door and let him in again. This time he just sat next to me on the sofa and, to be honest, with Kaz gone I found him a great comfort. I told him he might as well stay in for the night and went to bed.

At two or three o'clock in the morning I was woken by a tapping noise. Tap, tap, tap. I thought it must be a tap dripping and tried to ignore it by going back to sleep, but it went on for so long that eventually I sat up and turned the light on.

There was Denzil up on top of the chest of drawers, tapping on the urn with his paw. The hairs on the back of my neck stood straight up. I called to him to come down and leave the urn alone and he jumped down and went to the living room. The urn was too heavy for him to knock over, luckily.

After that he did it every night. Tap, tap, tap. I got so used to it that I'd just half wake up, say, 'Denzil, leave him alone,' and he'd jump down and curl up by me on the bed.

A few weeks into the new year I bought a life-sized statue of a white greyhound and put it in the back garden. And it became Denzil's statue. Every single day, come rain, wind or snow, for two whole years that cat kept up a vigil by the statue. He'd go out and lie next to it all day long, week in, week out. He defended it too – not even I was allowed anywhere near it. If I'd mown the lawn and got out a brush to whisk the grass cuttings off it, I'd hear a hissing and it'd be Denzil telling me to back off! Once I moved the statue and I looked up to see Denzil on the fence above me, ready to pounce! He was an exceptionally loving cat, so it was bizarre to see this aggressive side of his personality.

I got another rescue greyhound called Mac that first year and he and Denzil got on well, but if I let Mac out in the garden I had to muzzle him because if he went near Kaz's statue Denzil would hiss at him and get his claws out.

After two years Denzil, Mac, Kaz's statue and I moved out of the estate and off to Lanarkshire, where I would be able to keep more rescue greyhounds. As some of these dogs weren't safe with cats I knew I'd have to turn Denzil into a house cat and I wasn't sure how he'd take to that. Luckily, it turned out that he took to it like a duck to water – maybe because he was getting on a bit he seemed to have no interest in the outside world any more. It seemed to break the spell of the statue too. That went back out in the garden and he never asked to be let out to guard it. He just curled up with Mac and seemed to be as happy as Larry.

About eight months after we moved, Denzil started tapping me on the nose at what must have been about 5 a.m. I brushed him off and went on dozing, but minutes later Mac woke me up. He was really distressed and it was out of character for him to be up and about in the morning. Then I saw why.

He was running back and forth between me and the cat. Denzil was just lying on the floor on his side. I knew that something was very wrong right away. I tried to pick him up, but he was clearly hugely distressed.

We got him to the vet as soon as the surgery opened, just before 6 a.m., and it didn't take long to get a diagnosis. Denzil had suffered a massive stroke and was paralysed. I think he must have known it was coming and that was why he tried to wake me. I was warned that he had no chance of recovery. They left him for 12 hours to see if he improved, but when they squeezed his back legs with forceps to check for a reaction, there was none. Later I found out from a neighbour that Denzil had been hit by a car years ago and his old head injury had probably been the site of the stroke.

So I said, 'OK.' And took a deep breath. 'Denzil, give Mum a kiss.' He kissed my nose and I turned to the vet and said, 'OK, just put him to sleep now.' I knew he had somebody waiting for him.

He was the first cat I ever had, and I had him for such a short space of time. I'd always thought I was a doggy person and I never understood cats, but he changed my whole outlook. I'm glad his last two years were happy. We've got a memorial to him next to Kaz's statue. I've never found another cat like him.

CHAPTER FIVE

Animal Synchronicity

Spirit underwrites our lives, but most of us are so caught up in our own existence that we can't see it. If it does touch our awareness, it comes through a sudden moment of realization or an altered state, or perhaps a message from a medium. There's another way that spirit can make an impression on our day-to-day world, though, and that's 'synchronicity' – those coincidences and chains of events that are so striking that we're brought up short for a moment and think, 'Did that really happen? Was it *meant* to be like that? Why?'

I was taking part in a phone-in show on a BBC radio station once when a man told me a strange story. His wife had collected butterflies and at her funeral in midwinter an enormous and very rare butterfly had landed on her coffin and stayed with it until the committal. As the mourners walked out of the crematorium, it led the way, fluttering ahead of them. I knew I didn't need to explain what it meant to the widower; he had taken it for what it was: a sign from his wife that she was still with him. That's synchronicity – a 'coincidence' that really means something.

Several years ago I was taking part in a five-day seminar in Germany and one of the other participants was an incredible woman who must have been in her seventies, although you'd never have known it. She was an Apache who was a traditional healer and a medical doctor and had dedicated her life to using both means of healing to help people. She was full of wonderful stories and I loved to get her talking. We had some great discussions in the evening when the seminar work was over — I went on learning long after we'd finished all the workshops and talks! She was particularly interested in animals and the signs that are out there in the natural world for those who look for them and care to interpret them.

One of the participants at the seminar was a young man called Christian who seemed very agitated. During a coffee break he came over to talk to me, looking worried, and said he wanted to ask me some questions. He told me that he was due to travel to America in a short time but his grandfather was very ill and he was scared that if he went he would miss his passing and let him down. He thought I might be able to tell him, courtesy of spirit, when his granddad would leave this world.

I told him that wasn't the kind of information that the spirits usually gave me and tried to explain that it didn't matter if he wasn't physically with his grandfather as long as he made a mental connection with him. Christian didn't seem to be very reassured by this.

What I didn't know was that he'd been to talk to Mama Apache, too, and that she'd told him that there would be a sign when it was his granddad's time to cross over and that he should look out for it.

Two days before the end of the seminar I was out taking a walk round a lake near the retreat, and Christian, who was clearly still very troubled, came with me. It was dusk and there was a beautiful golden autumn light, with the leaves on the trees reflected in the water. Christian had been phoning home to find out what was happening, but there was no change in his grandfather's condition.

We'd been walking for about an hour and were turning for home when a fox crept out from behind a pine tree on the path ahead of us. In the golden light his red coat seemed golden too; he was a perfect part of the scene. He didn't seem at all perturbed by us, just trotted along calmly 10 yards ahead of us on the path. We fell silent, watching this gorgeous animal, and something in me told me the truth.

'Your grandfather's just gone over,' I said.

'How do you know?' asked Christian.

'I think that was the sign. If you phone home when we get back you'll find he's gone.' I don't know exactly how I knew, but I was 100 per cent sure.

When we got back to the retreat Christian called his parents and it was true: the old man had slipped away at the exact moment that the fox had appeared on the path. And the young man was a different person – instead of being devastated, he was relieved and uplifted. He told me, 'My grandfather found a way to let me know, even though I wasn't by his side. He sent that fox.'

When I saw Mama Apache later that evening the first thing she asked me was, 'Did you see your sign?'

I said, 'Yeah, the man's gone.'

And she said, 'Did you see a fox?'

'Yes!'

'Was it golden by any chance?'

'It was – it really looked golden.'

She told me that after talking to Christian she had done a meditation to help him and she'd sent him a golden fox.

This was puzzling, so I told her, 'But the fox we saw was real. It wasn't a spirit fox or some kind of apparition.'

And Mama Apache smiled and said, 'It doesn't matter how it appeared to you. The fact is that you received it and so did Christian, and you both understood the sign.'

She was happy. She had asked for a healing and the fox had been there to help. After that she called me Golden Fox, the person who dealt with the dead.

I can't draw on the same rich book of symbols that Mama Apache uses in her work, but I do have my own way of 'reading' the wildlife around me. You could call it 'ornithomancy' – divination by bird behaviour – but it's not something I'm even aware of doing half the time and I haven't got any set rules for it, like the old Roman or Celtic sages who used to watch the heavens for eagles and crows. I certainly don't go out in a headdress and start chanting till the birds come to me, but when certain birds appear in the sky it does tell me something. It's always some kind of bird of prey hovering overhead and it happens a lot when I'm travelling. I'll suddenly find my attention drawn to a piece of sky and I'll see it: a hawk or a harrier or a falcon. I could be in the middle of London and look up and see a kestrel. It happens when I'm preoccupied with something in my life and it's a way of letting me know that that problem is being answered or thought about by those in spirit. It's a sign of something higher than me, and not just literally! It's always reassuring and it always works. Those birds make me think of the greater side of existence, of beings looking at my little problems from a bigger perspective. That makes me feel much better.

Sometimes a pet arrives in our lives in a way that's as natural and as strange as one of those hawks over London or the butterfly in midwinter. It was obvious by the way that Charlie came into our lives with Dronma's sketch that there was a special reason for that dog arriving in our home. Cindy, the collie I owned with my wife when my boys were young, was a wonderful pet, but there was nothing extraordinary about the way she came to us and other than the fact that she was a joy to own, she didn't change my perspective on anything. Charlie hit the household like a bomb and demanded that we fitted our lives round him.

When I think back to Lassie, too, there were 10 of us lads out walking round Lumloch, but Lassie singled me out and then I had to figure out a way of keeping her when my mother hated pets. Sure enough, I've had an enduring psychic link with Lassie, as I'll explain later.

In cases like these there's a connection in consciousness between you and the animal that begins before you even meet. It's as if a contract's already been agreed, so there's no chance you will miss that opportunity to find them.

You'll be going on a journey together that'll be a big part of your life and it'll be a learning curve for both you and the animal. These special pets get caught up in dramas, illnesses or accidents, or sometimes they open new doors for us and change our lives. They inspire us to love them and to see their example and understand what a special being we've been linked to for a short while on this plane.

When Lois Hastings from Oxfordshire, in the heart of England, sent me her story about finding her dog Memphis in America, I knew this would turn out to be a real pet in a million:

I used to say to everyone that Memphis was never 'just a dog'. She definitely had a human consciousness and compared to other animals I'd had, she was unique in that respect. She was like a child in her awareness and had a far greater sense of self and personality than any other animal I'd met. She was stubborn, cheeky and strong-willed, just as a five-year-old might be. She loved doing things for the sheer enjoyment of it and was so spontaneous and in the moment: again, like a child would be.

I actually found her on a Hopi Indian reservation in America, one New Year's Eve, miles from anywhere. I got out of the car and there she was. It was an extremely spiritual place, even the land itself felt special, and I always felt that might have accounted for her spirituality.

She looked like a coyote but was jet black, and was about eight months old. She was totally tame. She sat down in front of me and announced silently that she was coming home with me, and that was that. From that time on she never left my side. I even said out loud to her, 'I know you,' as the connection was so strong. I couldn't even have a dog at that time, but that was immaterial! We literally thought as one mind, crazy as that might sound.

Memphis had such an awareness and understanding of the world around her and was very sensitive to different energies. If I was down, she was down. She was very sensitive to the bones and dried pigs' ears I would take home for her, which puzzled me at first. As much as she wanted to eat them, she would cry all the time, get distressed and eventually try to hide them out of sight down the back of the sofa. I finally decided she must somehow be feeling the dead animals' energy and stopped buying them for her. The same thing happened when she came across a lady's coat with rabbit-fur trim – she was really upset and cried, wanting to touch the fur but not being able to bear it, until I took it away and hid it from her.

At one time I lived on Long Island and used to drive into Manhattan every Friday evening at about 7 p.m. for the weekend. Memphis loved Manhattan and about lunchtime on a Friday she would be found curled up on the front seat of my car, patiently waiting until it was time to go, having jumped in through the open window.

Another time, when I was living in Santa Fe, we used to go hiking every weekend for hours at a time through woods and into the mountains. At one point I found a stick about three or four feet tall which I used as a staff for clambering across stepping stones and up hillsides. I wrapped string round one end to make it easier to grip and I used to take it home again after every outing.

One day I got fed up with holding it and left it by the side of a tree, propped up in the middle of a wood. Months later Memphis and I happened to be doing the same walk again and halfway through the hike she ran to the tree where the stick was and was so excited to have me reunited with my stick. She was jumping up, wagging her tail and running back to me to let me know she'd found it.

I still feel her jump on the bed when I'm going to sleep, even though she's been in the spirit world for four years now. She is still definitely making her presence felt!

She taught me a lot about having fun, being spontaneous and living in the moment. She also taught me patience and she definitely taught me that animals have a far greater degree of consciousness than most people realize, especially if you give them the space and encouragement to be themselves. Living in harmony with an animal rather than imposing our will upon them, as humans tend to do, allows their true personality to shine through. The strength of Memphis's personality amazed me — we didn't need words to communicate. She always let me know exactly how she felt.

Memphis reminded me of people like my brother, who could just never eat meat from when he was barely old enough to talk. We were brought up to eat and appreciate meat, but he just couldn't stomach it, even if it meant going hungry. I've since met many other vegetarians who are just like him; what began as pure instinct matured into an informed compassion for animals and an acute understanding of their suffering — exactly what Memphis had.

Memphis sounded like a teacher, and teachers come in all forms — sometimes on all fours! As the proverb says, when the student is ready the teacher appears. You just have to recognize them.

We have to identify the souls who come to guard us and to bring us joy, too. Reading about Brenda Cottingham's dog Heidi makes me think that this pet not only chose her home but also brought her family many moments of sheer delight. You'll see just what a character she was and how she managed to bring comfort even after she'd died.

My Weimaraner Heidi was something special from the beginning. We wanted to buy one of these beautiful grey 'ghost dogs' and had an interview with her breeder to see if we were suitable owners. When we went into the whelping shed we were warned not to touch the puppies as their mother was very protective, but when I knelt down on the floor one of the pups wiggled over and crawled onto my lap. That was Heidi. The mother came over and sniffed me, looked me right in the eye and then went back to her bed.

The owner said, 'That pup and her mother have chosen you,' and so began our mutual love affair.

Heidi really was a magical dog. Everybody loved her. You never knew what she was going to do next. She even used to queue at the local kebab stand and the owner would always give her her own kebab as a treat. If you took her to the beach you had to be prepared to stand there in wind, snow or rain because she adored the water.

Because she was bred to work and fetch game, I trained her to respond to hand signals and she could be very obedient despite her natural cheekiness.

Once she went racing across a frozen pond after a duck and fell in and I had to signal to her to swim back to me with her feet high and break the ice. She was shivering when she got home, so I gave her some hot chocolate, and after that she'd always try and get some more hot chocolate out of me by 'shivering' after a walk! She'd charm the birds off the trees if she thought she could persuade you to give her a treat!

She loved to chase game and almost caught up with some deer once, but she knew the difference between the rabbits on the heath and the pet rabbits in the pub garden – she'd stand nose to nose with them without attacking. I remember she was up to her belly in a pond once when a mother duck shot out from under the bank. I warned her, 'Now, Heidi, leave,' and she stood stock-still while 10 baby ducklings swam out after their mother and right under her nose. She looked at me as if to say, 'I hope no one's watching this!' but she didn't touch them.

She didn't like children, but would instinctively protect them. We were walking along a path by the Thames once where there was a steep drop down into the water. We passed a pub garden and Heidi was going on ahead when I saw a toddler heading towards the river. Her parents were chatting and hadn't noticed that she'd wandered off, but she was right near Heidi so I called to the dog and said, 'Mind the baby!'

Heidi looked at the toddler and got herself between her and the water and let the little girl put her arms round her. Then she gradually side-stepped away from the danger like a horse doing dressage, easing the child away. That's when the mother saw what was happening and I held my hand up to stop her shouting out. She understood and froze till I could get to Heidi and the baby.

I couldn't have let the mother try to take the baby herself because I knew Heidi took that 'Mind the baby!' command very seriously! I remembered being in the village chemist's once when a lady who'd just left came back into the shop and said, 'Excuse me, but is that your dog outside? The big grey one? It's just that she won't let me have my baby back.'

'Oh dear,' I said. 'Did you tell her to mind the baby?'

'Those were my exact words!' she said.

So we went out and there was Heidi by a pushchair and a baby was solemnly feeding her Smarties one by one. It turned out that every time the mother had tried to get near, Heidi had circled round and blocked her! She hadn't growled or bitten (she never bit a person) but just let the mother know she was minding the baby!

She was so protective of our family that my husband and son banned me from taking her to watch when they were windsurfing, because whenever they fell off their boards she'd be in the lake after them and she wouldn't leave them alone till they held onto her neck and pretended to let her swim them ashore and 'rescue' them!

Sadly, when she was just nine years old she was diagnosed with cancer of the spleen. She lasted six months, but then came a nightmare when she haemorrhaged at home and we had to rush her to the vet's for an operation. We had a sinking feeling that she might not make it through the procedure, so we made a big fuss of her and said our goodbyes in case it was the last time she was with us. The vet telephoned us later that day to tell us that there was nothing he could do, as poor Heidi was riddled with cancer. We went to say goodbye and I held her and she looked at me one last time. We were all heartbroken.

We brought her home and buried her in the garden. I was devastated and couldn't even go near the end of the garden where she lay. I lost all sense of proportion and worried that she'd get wet when it rained and that she was alone in spirit with no one that she knew. She was like a child to me. That was in January 1991.

About two weeks later in a dream my guide spoke to me and said, 'Brenda, Heidi is going on ahead,' and I immediately thought, 'Oh no,' because my father was in the early stages of Alzheimer's and he and Heidi had adored each other, so I thought that meant he was going to die.

I couldn't get back to sleep and was just lying there in bed wide awake when I felt a heavy weight jump onto the foot of the bed, then walk up towards me and turn round like Heidi used to and lie down. I reached out a hand and could feel her there, and after a while I felt her get up and walk down the bed and then I felt the thump as she jumped down onto the floor. Quickly I turned on the light but of course there was nothing there.

A week later at 6 a.m. my niece's husband telephoned me from the hospital to say that my brother-in-law Barry had had a heart attack at the age of 54 and the outlook was hopeless. We rushed over there and I sat by his head and he opened his eyes and spoke to me, then closed them again. Later in the day when I was in the waiting room looking after my niece's child so that she could be with her father, a nurse called us and said we had better come, but it was too late and Barry had passed over. I was devastated, as we had been very close and he had been another person on Heidi's 'favourites' list.

A few nights later I had a dream of Barry throwing sticks in the large field where he used to walk Heidi when he looked after her when we were on holiday. I had this dream many times after that and it was always the same – Heidi would be racing after the sticks and bringing them back to him.

One night as the same dream was playing out, I called to Heidi and instead of running back to Barry she came racing towards me but stopped halfway. She stood looking at me and then turned to look at Barry, who called her. With one last glance at me, she went back to him. He waved at me and they both turned and walked away. Heidi had found someone to be with in spirit. After that I never dreamed of Heidi or 'felt' her on the bed again.

Years later I persuaded my husband John to go to one of Gordon's theatre readings in Margate because although he'd known me for over 30 years and knew that I was a medium, he still didn't believe that messages could come through from the other side. He'd find all sorts of excuses!

John's brother-in-law Derrick had passed a month before and that night Gordon brought him through and John couldn't believe it. Then Gordon said, 'And I've got a big grey dog here and she's bounding over to you,' and John said, 'That's Heidi,' and there were tears running down his face. Gordon went on, 'And there's a little dog here as well, a feisty one, and she wants to come as well.' And that was John's own dog, Judy.

That convinced him. I couldn't believe it – over the years I'd brought through his mother, his father and his grandparents, but he hadn't believed me till Gordon brought Heidi back to us!

How could a personality like Heidi not come back? By hook or by crook she was going to get herself known that night at the theatre, and that strength of self had nothing to do with her species. She could have been a man, a cat or a gerbil and she would still have got her message across! I bet she's still guarding her family, here and in spirit, and still making them laugh too.

I've found it very common for animals in spirit to become the link which draws human spirits into connection with a medium or loved one. They instinctively know to go to a medium, whereas a human spirit might not understand how. Heidi cemented the evidence for John, adding a little more proof so he could understand about life after death and feel better about his brother-in-law's death.

There are lots of examples of animals that seem to choose a particular individual, even when they are new to a home and have a whole family there to spoil them. It doesn't have to be a big spiritual happening, with dreams and synchronicity, it can be as simple as a cat heading straight for one person's lap. Ultimately, animals are like humans in this respect. Some people are good at assessing the folk around them and are attracted to someone who will be a lifelong friend. They will hang back and watch everyone and then approach the person they think is going to understand them best.

A lot of animals who have a higher consciousness, like Charlie, are just like that – they are wary and will pick carefully. Ultimately, they're showing an instinct to love and be loved – they know who's going to defend them and they want to return that affection.

You can see how strong that instinct is by the way lots of animals can be very quick to forgive, especially dogs. I think cats are less forgiving on the whole because they have a more discerning instinct than dogs do – they're the ones who are more likely to choose a 'special person'. Dogs might choose someone because they're the pack leader, but I think cats pick friends, pure and simple.

You never see cats on those TV programmes for badly behaved animals, because it's dogs that get confused when they have no pack leader and start acting dominantly. Cats already know they're in charge! This story from South African Astrid Wareham just goes to show that even when a cat is in no position to choose its protectors, it'll still manage it somehow.

I've always had a pack of cats about the house and I'm notorious among my friends for taking in strays. There was a little ginger boy cat who seemed to be living in the car park at the place where I worked and the company had adopted him. People brought him food every day. Once someone took him home, but he ran away the next day and reappeared in the car park. He was happy with being wild. I gave him the odd treat, but kept my distance, as I felt he didn't want anything more than that.

One day I found him lying in my path. I don't know why the hundreds of other people who walked there every day hadn't seen him, as there he was, unable to move. He definitely looked worse for wear. I gently picked him up and took him to the vet, who checked him over and told me he had a broken pelvis.

After that I took Redge — short for 'Redgetable' because of his carrot-coloured coat — home and nursed him night and day till he recovered. Two weeks after he was back on his feet and eating well, he started vomiting and continued for days. I took him back to the vet, who found an obstruction in his intestine — scar tissue from whatever had happened to him previously. We suspected that someone had injured him badly, which would explain how scared he was of people. The vet said he could operate, but it would be expensive.

I agonized over the money. It would cost more than I could afford and hurt us financially as a family, but things were happening so fast that before I knew it the op was done and the bill was on its way! The vet told me they'd done what they could and it was up to Redgie whether he was going to survive or not. The day after his operation I sat with him in the animal hospital. The poor little cat was on a drip, wrapped in bandages and with a long scar down his stomach.

I talked to him and told him it was up to him now, we'd brought him this far and he had to do the rest. It can't have been easy for him, with his fear of people. I held my hands over him and prayed for healing.

A week later he had recovered enough to go home with us and although I was relieved, I was also apprehensive about the cost of the whole procedure. I had to pay off his medical bills now! I'd put it all on my credit card.

Less than a month later, before the first payment had been deducted, a friend took me for a girly night out at the local casino. I was very reluctant to play, but didn't want to spoil everyone's fun. I couldn't really afford to stake a lot, but I stood in front of a slot machine and began playing it absentmindedly. I wasn't even watching what it was doing and had my head turned away so I could talk to my friends, when suddenly the machine seized up. Then it began telling me I'd won lots of money!

I won a large amount that day; it covered the cost of Redgie's medical bills and there was a little left over. I cried tears of joy and was very humbled by this. God and my angels talk to me all the time, but this was spectacular even by my standards!

Redgie is learning to trust people again and we love his quirky little personality. He'll come and sit by me when I'm reading or painting, even though he spends most of the day hiding till I come home from work.

I think this a real case of 'pennies from heaven' and yes, it's synchronicity playing its tricks again. Very often when we need help so that another can benefit, the cosmic cash machine pays out – literally, in Astrid's case!

My last story is about another kind of direct message – this time from a human loved one. About a year ago I'd just finished a book signing and had popped out for a cigarette. One of the ladies who'd been in the bookshop came out to join me and after we'd had a little chat about the weather, she asked me if she could tell me about something that had happened to her, so I said, 'Of course.'

'What do you think of this?' she asked, and then explained that her husband had died a couple of years before and had gone very quickly, so she'd never had a chance to say goodbye. Almost a year to the day later, she'd had an amazing dream about him which had been strangely vivid. In it she'd been in her own kitchen and her husband had opened the back door and walked in just as he had in life after work – he'd worked as a builder and had often been covered in mud and dust after a long day on the site, so she used to make him come round through the garden so he didn't mess up the carpet. This time, instead of walking up to her for a kiss, he'd pushed the door open even wider and a cat had come padding in. It had been jet black with white paws and a white spot on its nose. It had strolled right up to her, leapt onto her knee and cuddled her, and then her husband had smiled and laughed and walked back out of the door. Then she had woken up.

A few days later she had been in the kitchen when she had suddenly heard meowing, so she had gone to the back door and opened it and in had walked a jet-black cat with white paws and a white spot on its nose. And it had started to rub itself against her leg and purr. She'd checked it for a collar, but it didn't have one – it was as though it had appeared out of thin air.

She'd never had a cat in her life, but this new friend didn't seem bothered. He just moved in and made himself at home. She called him 'Five Spots' because of his markings.

When she'd finished telling me about Five Spots she asked me if I thought he was a gift from her husband. I replied, 'Well, do you think it's a gift from him?' and she said without a shadow of doubt, 'Yes, I feel it was. I think that was him coming to me in the dream and bringing me that cat.'

CHAPTER SIX

~

People Who Can
Talk to the Animals

Every Scottish schoolchild learns the true story of the little Skye terrier who was nicknamed Greyfriars Bobby. Bobby was the watchdog of a policeman called John Gray who had his beat in one of the poorest parts of Edinburgh, and when his master died of tuberculosis, Bobby was distraught. He followed the funeral procession to the Greyfriars graveyard and had to be picked up and carried away from the graveside. Back at the rooms where his family lived, he howled all through the funeral tea, and that night he escaped and ran back to his master. He stayed by John Gray's unmarked grave for 14 years, keeping vigil just as he'd been taught as a police dog. Locals got to know the dog well and would coax him into their houses on the coldest nights and he got a free meal every day from a local temperance inn, but he always went back to his master's side.

Most people think that Bobby's the most fascinating character in this story and his loyalty was staggering, but I'm more intrigued by John Gray, about whom very little is known. He had inspired that devotion in the little dog long after he'd left this world and even when the dog had plenty of other friendly people willing to care for him. For something that singular to happen, you need to be quite an exceptional person and have great empathy with animals.

I never met Ralph Cockburn's mother, Ann Heron, but she must have had that empathy in order to kindle the love her dog Heidi obviously felt for her. Ralph tells the story:

In August 1990 my mother was murdered while she was sunbathing in the garden of her house in a village outside Darlington, a case which is still unsolved and which has been widely reported in the media. She had a rough collie called Heidi who was always at her side and whom she'd had since she was a puppy, and one of the mysteries of what happened that day is that Heidi disappeared for a few hours after my mother was killed, and for a shy but devoted dog that was extraordinary. She returned a few hours later, when my mother's body had been discovered and the police had arrived.

She was only a young dog – just three years old – but she died two weeks later. You can't tell me she wasn't broken-hearted.

Some people don't appreciate animals or think nothing of treating them cruelly. They're fixed on their own games in life and don't look outside their box – they think animals are there to be used for their benefit or to be ignored or abused. Then there are people who do love animals, but only if they can turn them into something more 'human', which is like forcing your own personality on another creature and expecting it to reflect you back to yourself like a mirror. There's another type of person, too, who notices much more about the life surrounding them and lets it be, and they tend to be attractive to animals. These people are usually capable of taking on a dog and letting it be 100 per cent dog or giving the animal a job that shapes its nature, like guarding something or sniffing out drugs. I'd guess John Gray was one of these individuals.

People who have true empathy with animals used to be looked on as dangerous and spooky – 'witches' with 'familiars' who might be shunned, or worse, by those around them. I think you are still considered a bit 'weird' if you appear to be 'too close' to a pet. The thing is, though, that anyone who's considered fey is likely to be more in tune with nature in the first place and so would recognize the character of their animal to a greater degree. Their cat, for example, would be their buddy, their best friend, and they would accept that they were not just a cat but a conscious living being that needed to be treated with respect and compassion. In days gone by a person like this would have been seen as someone who charmed animals. In fact, it was the other way round: the animals charmed the person. Nothing supernatural about it.

All kinds of animals just gravitate towards these people, knowing they'll be acknowledged as beings in their own right and cared for. My friend Dronma is a great example; she just has an overwhelming appreciation of animals, and as a Buddhist who ends her prayers with the wish that 'all beings be happy' she's extending her compassion to all life forms every day. She doesn't measure one against another – the barriers between the species are down for her and everything is appreciated for its own sake.

Dronma is one of those people who just instinctively has the trust of all species. I remember when she kept bees she would walk up and down the street with her swarm floating around her head, keeping her company! She can stand in a field and deer will come right up to her. Her philosophy is, 'If they don't bother me, I won't bother them,' and it's served her well. She told me once that when she was painting in the desert in Arizona she had rattlesnakes slithering round her feet.

When she was pregnant with her daughter, she had a cat who was also expecting. They used to take an afternoon rest together, with the cat lying on Dronma's bump. When Dronma was about eight months pregnant, the cat gave birth. One day while Dronma was having a snooze upstairs, the cat appeared, carrying one of her kittens. She jumped onto the bed and put the kitten on Dronma's belly. Then she jumped down and trotted out.

Dronma picked up the kitten and went to carry it back to its basket, but met the cat on the stairs, bringing up a second kitten. Dronma put both kittens back in their bed downstairs and went back for a lie-down, but the cat reappeared with another kitten in her mouth and laid it on her. This time my friend decided that the cat obviously had something in mind, so she just lay still while the cat went up and down the stairs until she had fetched all the kittens and parked them on Dronma's belly. Then she went out and did a spot of hunting or whatever her business was, and came back and picked up the kittens one by one. Obviously she trusted Dronma so much that she had decided she could do the babysitting!

Animals like cats and dogs that are sentient enough to open up to another species and allow us to domesticate them have a kind of radar for someone like Dronma, which is something like a telepathic ability. It travels along the same bonds of connection.

To be trusted by an animal, as my friend was by her cat, means that they have sensed that you have empathy with them and have accepted you into their lives. Animals can trust very quickly and won't spend ages wondering if they were right or wrong about that decision. They'll trust until you do something that breaks that trust, and in the case of some dogs, they'll still go on trusting even then. They certainly don't waste time wondering how other animals will judge that decision!

Any breach of that trust is on *our* part, not theirs. It's very rare to hear of an animal who has turned on a person 'for no reason', unless it's one of those poor 'devil dogs' who's had aggression bred and trained into it. Usually a dog will love you and try to show you that they love you even if you beat or hurt them – and even then they'll try and apologize to you. They'll be upset that the love they are trying to communicate is not being understood. No wonder they're so happy when they find a person who can appreciate them.

If you take in animals and give them a new human family, you take them on a radically different journey and their instincts and behaviour have to change to fit in with you. They may do things that are right according to their way of thinking but that earn them a smack or a telling-off from a human. We may give them the wrong body language or confuse them by allowing them to be dominant, then eating our meals before they eat theirs.

You might say you have a cat that's anti-social or a dog that never pays attention to people, but you'd be wrong – they've just learned that humans aren't interested in them, so they don't bother!

How do you make that connection with an animal? Often it's just a matter of taking time. I don't believe that certain people have an inborn ability to talk to the animals, it's just that some people take more time to understand and observe them.

I sit down with Meg and watch her ears and her expressions and how she tilts her head to listen. Why should an animal have to 'think' in human words when they already have a subtler and more beautiful language for communication? And if you find ways to communicate with animals and take them seriously as fellow beings, then you will get to know their hurts, their fears and feelings, and they'll appreciate the connection that you offer them.

Anna O'Callaghan from County Meath in Ireland had a son who was a quiet, sensitive young man and who, like Dronma, could truly 'talk' to animals.

My son Martin always loved animals and right from a very young age all he wanted was to be a vet so he could help them. He had a special way with animals; they'd just walk up to him and he could identify with them. I'd see him approach a wild, snarling dog and when it saw him it would just stop and let him pat it. When he was growing up he had a little white Jack Russell called Snowy who was with us for 16 years and whom he loved more than life.

He was partway through his degree and doing practice with a vet when he heard about a dog called Sparky who needed a new home. The collie belonged to a farmer but he'd been chasing cattle on the farm and now he was chained up outside the house and was four days away from being put down by his owner. Martin persuaded him to give him Sparky and the dog was completely devoted to him.

Because Martin was away at college four days a week, my husband and I looked after Sparky for him, but every Friday come 3:30 p.m. the dog would jump up onto a bench in the garden and stare through the back window, waiting for the moment when Martin arrived through the front door. He wouldn't move till he saw him. You could stand in his way and he'd look round you; you could offer him food and he wouldn't take it. He'd wait there for three hours till his master came home. All he cared about was seeing Martin, and if my son played a game and pretended not to see the dog when he arrived, Sparky would tap on the window till he noticed him.

Martin was always very bright and sensitive, but he suffered badly from depression and he pushed himself very hard trying to help everyone. He was a member of the Dublin Society for the Prevention of Cruelty to Animals, and he was hoping that when he qualified as a vet he could dedicate his life to caring for animals in need. He sometimes took medication, but when he got better he would assure me he was as bright as a button and would try to do without the pills. Then he would get very low again and push everyone away and promise them he was fine.

When he was low, Sparky would become very protective of him. If I tried to rub Martin's shoulders or stroke his head, Sparky would put himself between us and push me away, then put a paw on each of Martin's shoulders and lower his own head so it was next to my son's.

A few months before Martin was due to complete his degree, Sparky suddenly started barking every evening, long into the night. At first we thought it was because of the fireworks — it was round about the end of October and the beginning of November — but he kept on barking for weeks, right into December, and it was driving us demented. Sparky was a quiet dog normally, so it was completely out of character.

My grandmother always said that dogs barked when someone was going to die and I think Sparky was doing it then because there were a lot of spirits coming to the house to be with the family. Martin took his own life that December, nine weeks before he would have taken his final exams. He had gradually been getting sicker and sicker over the last few months and although his doctor had thought he would improve soon, the anti-depressants he was taking weren't enough to help him.

The morning that Martin was leaving the house to be buried, Sparky was out the back in the garden with three rooms between him and his master, but he howled and howled and howled, looking up at the sky. My husband had to leave the coffin to go back to him and try to calm him down.

At the wake, if anyone went into the garden who was wearing cords – which Martin always wore – Sparky growled at them. He is a beautiful, placid dog and he's never done anything like it since.

A few days after the funeral, my other son Fergal decided to take Sparky to the cemetery to see if he would be any different or could sense where Martin had gone. I drove them there and when we got out, Fergal put Sparky on a lead and said he'd just let the dog go wherever he chose. The dog pulled him straight to Martin's grave, sat at the foot and turned his back to the headstone. He sat there and just gazed up to the sky again. He will not go to the grave now if we take him to the cemetery, no matter how much we coax him.

Now my husband likes to walk Sparky and it's been good for us to have him with us – he gets us out of the house and helps us to cope. He's all we have left of Martin.

Martin is still with us, though, and has given us evidence that he is around. Eight weeks after he died the Society for the Prevention of Cruelty to Animals in Dublin erected a plaque in his memory and I went along to unveil it. Before he passed, Martin had had a petition from Lourdes which he had carried with him all the time and it had listed everything he wanted to do. First was raising money for the DSPCA.

My husband took lots of photos of the unveiling ceremony, which we sent off to be developed. I was a bit disappointed when I received them because there was a shadow to one side of the plaque and I couldn't read what the engraving said. A year later I became curious and took two of the photos to a photo shop and asked them to zoom in on the plaque and enlarge it for me. Lo and behold, whenever I show it to anyone who knew my son, they tell me the shadow is the image of Martin's face.

I then investigated the other photos on the contact sheet and in one there seemed to be a white shape on the plaque. It's very strange, but if you view the contact sheet with a magnifying glass you can see that the white blur is the image of Snowy, Martin's first dog.

A couple of weeks ago I was going away for the weekend and I very deliberately told Martin that if he was visiting us, he must move a picture in the house to let us know he was there. When I came back I was up on a stepladder dusting the light in Fergal's room when I noticed that a photo in a heavy frame that normally hung on one of the walls was now perched on top of the door jamb. I called Fergal and asked him why he'd put it there — it could have fallen on someone coming into the room — but he was as puzzled as me. My husband didn't know anything about it either. I wonder who moved it.

Sometimes strange things happen, like the faces appearing on the photos and the picture moving, and it's up to us whether or not we question them. But if these things have happened and have been understood as communications from spirit, why doubt them? I bet that Sparky wouldn't for a minute.

I spoke to Vicky Wade from Oregon, USA, on a Hay House radio show, when she called in to tell me about an unusual pet who was still making her presence felt and whose bond with her husband had been profound.

Stella was the last kid of triplets to be born and my husband and I had just arrived back from a trip into town to buy more goat food when her mother, Amber, pushed her into the world. Stella was a Nubian goat and she was pure black with a small white blaze on her forehead and a diamond-shaped spot on her chest. I wrapped her in a towel and handed her to my husband, Bob, who lay on the floor and gently wiped her dry, stroking her and soothing her with his soft voice. She quietened down and then fell asleep on him.

Because she was one of three, we were bottle-feeding her from the very beginning and she soon grew totally attached to Bob. She had a different bleat from any of our other goats and if my husband ever went out of her sight she'd screech for him! When she was only two weeks old she slid under the wood heater in the living room to sleep in the warmth, with her head poking out from under it, so that when she opened her eyes she'd see Bob. If he went outside for anything, she'd scramble out and follow him, and if it was raining she'd stand on the porch and screech for him to come back indoors. I would have to tell her it was OK and he'd be back, and then she'd calm down.

We had erected a wire gate across the hallway to our bedroom because we needed our sleep without one of the goats jumping on the bed in the night, as we never closed the door. Stella would keep watch from the hall, where she would lie on a big throw pillow. When Bob was recovering from a partial amputation, we installed a big-screen television at the foot of the bed and Stella would watch the telly with him until she fell asleep. She'd be there all night and would wait for him to wake in the morning.

Theirs was a mutual love. As far as Bob was concerned, Stella could do no wrong. When he worked under one of the vehicles she would get down on her knees beside him and peer underneath to see what he was doing. He'd laugh and pet her, kissing and nuzzling her face, and she'd be thrilled. She would wag her tail, kick her heels and jump and run in circles after him. The more he laughed, the more she would show off.

When he sat at the table in his den to play solitaire, Stella would sit in the chair opposite him and shuffle his cards with her nose. She never ate them, just pushed them around. Much of her leisure time was spent curled up on a rug by his chair. He would casually reach down, even when he was reading a magazine, and stroke her soft fur. They were just content to be together.

The night Stella died from a mineral deficiency that caused liver and kidney failure, Bob and I were both devastated.

Tears flowed freely. We wrapped her in a new blanket and quietly laid her in the ground, placing a marker to identify her resting place.

For days afterwards, Bob's thoughts were of Stella and he would choke up just speaking about her. The joy had gone out of his games of solitaire. He seemed to feel her presence at the table but finally gave up playing, he missed her so much.

One morning, a few weeks later, while seated by the wood heater and drinking his morning cup of coffee, he felt a warm nudge against the back of his trouser leg, right where Stella used to lean against him. His face was a picture of shock and disbelief.

'I think Stella is here,' he quietly remarked. 'Is it possible?' We had been discussing the subject of whether or not animals had souls or were able to contact us after death.

'Sure,' I said. 'Acknowledge her presence by petting her as you used to.'

He hesitantly reached down and stroked the unseen fur. At the same time, Daffodil, one of our six-month-old twin goats, leaned forward and pressed her forehead against his other knee. She, too, missed Stella and helped Bob acknowledge her presence.

We know Stella is still with us, communicating from the other side, and it lessens our grief. We know she was not an ordinary goat, but came to carry Bob through a difficult time and help him to heal.

Sometimes I hear him talking to Stella as if she were physically present and there are still times when I am preparing dishes of food for the other pet goats and I 'feel' Stella at my elbow, watching me slice the apples, carrots and bananas. When I throw in a few grapes, I can sense she is licking her lips in anticipation of her favourite food.

Vicky was more than convinced that her husband's experience was real, and I think she was doubly moved because he was quite sceptical and not the kind of man to talk about something like that, but he couldn't deny that Stella had been back, nor that he'd been delighted to have her there.

⌐

CHAPTER SEVEN

~

Telepathy

I was half-asleep in an armchair at home and suddenly it felt as though the chair was shaking and I was lifted up out of myself. The first thing I saw as I looked down on my body in the armchair was Lassie, my red setter, and then I was in a landscape like the pheasant fields, and a mass of animals was coming over the hill like a Pedigree Chum advert, every kind of animal you could think of, and I had the extraordinary feeling that I wasn't afraid of the animals, and they weren't scared of me, and it felt like a grand reunion. I haven't got any other way to describe this tremendous feeling. It was just an amazing scene and it felt completely real, as though it was actually happening and I was there in the pheasant fields. Better still, we could all communicate directly with each other – it was like a Disney film or something and there I was in the middle, being Dr Doolittle!

I think if I learned anything from that experience it was that you don't really need to speak to communicate. Although the animals and I were almost silent, there was more to hear and understand in that silence that in all the communications we humans are forever trying to make with our mobile phones and e-mails.

I've talked a lot about telepathy being an impulse of feeling and one that can jump across time as well as between animal and human consciousness, but what is it actually like to experience that message? My out-of-body experience gave me an idea, but you don't have to be in a kind of trance to feel it, and it's a humbling experience when it happens.

A few years ago I went on a trip to South Africa with my son Paul and we visited a game reserve. The highlight was the chance to meet one of the reserve's cheetahs. There were two of these magnificent cats in a pen and the keeper asked if anyone wanted to stroke one of them. The male was huge, taller than a greyhound, with a thin flat tail with a fluffy end and that small cheetah head held high. He was called Lord Byron. The keeper said that if we did approach him, we shouldn't be nervous and we should avoid looking him straight in the eye at all costs because he would think that was a challenge. 'Approach him from behind,' he said. 'If you walk up to him from the front he'll think you're challenging him and then he'll pounce and it'll all be over.'

I edged into the pen with Paul, keeping my head down, and stood beside the cat. I stood near his ears but not too close, and the keeper said encouragingly, 'Stroke him. Stroke his back.' So I put out a hand tentatively and ran it along the bony spine. The cat turned its head slowly and I kept my head down. He went on staring at me, checking me out, and the keeper said, 'React! Do something, but keep your head down.' Eventually the cat turned away and let me go on stroking him. Then he started purring like a giant kitten. Poor Paul was terrified!

That cat was incredible, though. He just gave off this tremendous sense of self and if you approached him you were most definitely in his zone and not the other way round. I had nothing but respect for him, for his wildness, his innocence.

To me the power and sense of self that he gave off were pure telepathy and I responded, just trying to send out lovely thoughts to him – 'You're beautiful, you're so calm' – because I knew he could read my emotions. Animals react to every shade of emotion and as a medium I've had a lot of practice in checking my own feelings – if I want to cry, for instance, is that my own emotion or one that's coming through from spirit?

How can you develop that telepathic link with animals for yourself? First you have to forget that it's something to do with thought. Don't think, 'Come here,' because that won't work. You have to really *want* the dog or cat to be with you. They pick up on your emotions – your happiness, your fear. That's how they 'know' when you need them, and that's the purest form of telepathy. Even the word 'telepathy' comes from *telos*, 'far away' or 'remote', and *patheia*, which means 'affected by' or 'experienced', rather than 'thought'. We are definitely capable of telepathy – think of how often you can pip on the fact that someone's angry for example – it's just something that's emitted, even if the person in question is trying to deny mentally that they're upset.

Even though we all have this telepathic ability, though, so often we try to use logic to explain what we're picking up, and that doesn't work. I was on tour in Italy once and had just gone up to my hotel room and put my head on the pillow when I suddenly heard yelping and whining. I sat bolt upright. It sounded exactly like Charlie. I was almost confused enough to look for him at the end of the bed. It was so loud and so real, it didn't sound as though it was coming from inside my head at all. I lay back again, wondering what it could be, and then I heard it start up once more. I immediately reached for the phone by the bed and dialled Jim, who was a bit surprised that I was phoning at midnight.

'Is Charlie all right?'

'Well, he didn't eat his dinner and he's looking a little sorry for himself.'

'Listen, you've got to take him to the vet as soon as you can.' I told him about the whimpering and yelping that I'd heard and that I was sure there was something really wrong with the pup.

Jim wasn't convinced it was that urgent. 'I'm sure he's OK really. I expect he ate something wrong out on a walk and he'll sick it up and be all right in no time. I'll leave it tonight and see how he is in the morning.'

Reluctantly I let it drop and tried to get some sleep. But in the morning I woke up with an excruciating stomach ache and I knew it was nothing to do with the previous night's dinner! It was a God-awful feeling, really ominous. I phoned Jim again.

'How's Charlie?'

'He's not bouncing around, but he doesn't look too bad.'

'Look, you've got to take him to the vet.'

'I've got too much to do and you should see him – he's really not bad at all. Whatever it is will probably go through his system and he'll be fine in no time.'

I couldn't let this happen, 'Seriously, I mean it. He's telling me something is wrong. Maybe it doesn't show from the outside, but it's really bad.'

In the end Jim said he'd take him to the vet. It turned out that Charlie *had* eaten something bad for him out on a walk – two huge stones. He always picked up stones to chew on and this time he'd swallowed a couple whole: there they were on the X-rays, sitting in his stomach like bombs. The sharper one had cut through the lining of his stomach and his stomach acid was seeping out. The vet rushed him straight into theatre to remove them. Afterwards he told us that Charlie would have died in great pain in a short period of time if he hadn't operated there and then. He was also amazed at the size of the stones. We kept them for years and no one could understand how Charlie had managed to swallow them in the first place!

How could I have known that something was wrong from so far away? The psychic connection we have with our pets is strong and it's no different from the one we have with our human loved ones. If a person is in pain or trouble, even if they are out of our sight, if there's a connection of love it allows us to reach out to them in emotional or painful times.

Charlie managed to send his actual voice, so that I could hear him whimpering, but your inner ear isn't the only sense that can be reached by animal telepathy. Eleni Barbetsea-Baillie of Castle Douglas in Scotland had a precious white cat who was a very adept communicator, and when he got into trouble he had a direct line to his owner!

When I was growing up in Athens I had a lovely white tomcat called Zizikos. I'd known his mother Zouzou for most of my life, as she belonged to someone in our old apartment building, and she was definitely a unique character. She was also white with one blue eye and one green. When my family moved away, Zouzou's owner promised my sister and me one of her kittens because I'd been so attached to the cat and so we came to have Zizikos, who was very, very young when he arrived.

Every cat is unique and you have to build a different relationship with each one. They're like people, you can't compare them and they're all irreplaceable. Zizikos had or chose to have a closer attachment to me than to my sister and he trusted me absolutely. He'd even let me wash him in the bath when he got grubby, which happened quite often because of his colouring.

When I went to bed he would hide and wait till everything was quiet and my mother had gone to sleep before jumping onto the cover or even snuggling underneath it in the winter.

He knew my mother didn't approve of cats in beds! He liked to escort me to the bus when I went to university in the morning and I could talk to him and hold entire conversations. He had different meows with different meanings, one for food, one for affection and so on.

He was always very communicative and very responsive to attention. I taught him to jump through hoops and to leap up to my outstretched arm and swing on it like a monkey. He liked to have me watch him balancing on the narrow ledge of our balcony, just to show off and say, 'Look at me!' He could also sense the mood of everyone in the family and behave accordingly. If my brother, who didn't like him, was in a bad mood, he'd adapt his behaviour or come to me for protection. We were very close.

In the autumn of 1981 the family moved to a new flat on the third floor of a block several miles away from our old home. Zizikos appeared to be happy enough there, but one day, as cats do, he decided to take off, and vanished. I was still at university and I can recall vividly that I could not rest or concentrate on my work while my little fluffy white boy was missing. All I cared about was knowing where he'd gone.

How can you find a cat in a city of five million people? Anything could have happened to him, a car accident probably. But Zizikos was a streetwise cat in the big city, so I searched and searched and talked to people in the neighbourhood and beyond. He was part of the family, part of my life.

One day about two weeks later I woke up in tears after a powerful dream. I told my sister all about it. I'd seen a huge wall and Zizikos was on the other side of it, his paws raised up to me, begging me to reach down for him. He was meowing loudly.

My dreams have always meant a lot to me and I often let them guide what I do in real life. And that night it was as though the dream images were magnified. I recognized the wall too, as it separated our old house from the next-door neighbour's. Zizikos was trying to communicate to me where he was.

I didn't waste any time and went immediately to the old house. When I went to look over the wall that separated the two houses I looked down and saw the very same image as in my dream: Zizikos reaching up with his paws and meowing at me. He'd obviously gone back to look for me and been confused that I wasn't in the old house, and then he'd told me where he was, so I could come and find him.

After that we became even closer. Sadly, Zizikos didn't have the chance to live his full life cycle, as a year or so later he was killed by a local woman who hated animals and fed meat with ground glass in it to several of the cats and dogs in our neighbourhood. My sister and I came home to find Zizikos waiting for us, and he was bleeding badly. I held him like a baby, and that's when he let go and died. The pain is still vivid even 20 or more years later, but I know in my heart that Zizikos's spirit is still with me.

The bond between Eleni and Zizikos was obviously so strong that he could impress himself on her mind when he was lost.

It certainly wouldn't take him long to connect mind-to-mind from the other side if he felt she needed him now, but I think the fact that they were so connected in real life would help his spirit advance on the other side. He's not going to worry, being a cat. He has done his job and he won't keep coming back to say he's fine — Eleni's faith means he doesn't have to. It strikes me that their friendship was complete from the start — they really were kindred souls.

Roy McKeag's collies Sonny and Bess had a similar bond with their human protector, so much so that when Bess got into trouble Roy knew exactly how to reach out to her:

I used to say that Sonny, Bess and I could read one another's minds. I had proof, too. One day over the Christmas and New Year's holidays I took the two dogs for a walk in a very large forest managed by the Forestry Commission. It covered a vast area and had many dirt roads criss-crossing through the trees. We had often gone there for walks, and I knew some of the roads that followed a string of small lochs, but the other roads were just a maze to me.

The trees were planted very close together, as they were being grown for timber, and there wasn't much light if you took a step or two off the paths. As we walked along, a rabbit suddenly jumped out of the trees, saw the dogs and disappeared back into the forest. Sonny and Bess set off in hot pursuit. They loved to chase the rabbits that lived in the field at the bottom of my garden for fun, although they never caught or harmed them, so this rabbit was too tempting to leave!

Within seconds both dogs had vanished into the dense plantation and I began to worry. I called out their names and tried to follow them, but the branches of the trees were too thick and I would have had to crawl on my hands and knees to get through. The ground was thick with undergrowth. After a couple of minutes Sonny burst out of the wood and onto the road with a smile on his face, but Bess was nowhere to be seen.

I stood there a while calling her, but my voice was bounced back by the impenetrable trees. I knew there was another road running parallel to the one I was on, so after 30 minutes I thought I'd make my way round there to see if she had emerged on the other side. It took me another 30 minutes to get there, but Bess was nowhere to be seen. The light was fading and I was extremely worried. It was the middle of winter and she couldn't stay out all night. I kept peering into the trees and shouting, and eventually it became completely dark.

I had no option but to retrace my steps to the car park a couple of miles away. At one point I turned a corner and was surprised to see a forestry worker with a chainsaw running — the trees were so dense that the sound of it hadn't even travelled 100 or so yards. There was little chance that Bess could have heard my shouts.

I had no idea what to do next. The forest was 30 miles from my home and I had to be at work by 8:30 a.m. the next morning. It was a Sunday and nowhere was open. I'd probably have to take the Monday off work and return to put up posters and go to the nearest police station, which was three miles away.

When I got back to my car I realized that the gate to the forest road, which was normally closed, had been left open. Private cars weren't allowed to drive in the forest, but the worker must have forgotten to close it off, so with the car on full-beam headlights I set off again down the pitch-black forest roads.

I drove for hours, but there wasn't a sign of Bess. Eventually I turned up the long and winding road where she had disappeared, switched the engine off and sat there in the darkness. I feverishly sent out thoughts telling Bess I was there and I would wait for her. I got out of the car and sat on the bonnet and continued to send out thoughts.

After about 15 minutes I got cold and was about to climb back into the car with Sonny when somehow I knew that Bess had got my message and that I needed to stay out a little longer, so I stayed outside frantically shouting, 'Here, Bess!' in my head.

Another 15 minutes passed and I thought I saw a black shadow a long way back on the road behind me. The road was too narrow to turn the car round and use the headlights to light it, so I waited and then suddenly there she was, a bedraggled and exhausted but relieved Bess.

I hugged her and felt we were holding a telepathic conversation. I felt that she told me she had only chased the rabbit for a minute or so, then realized that Sonny wasn't around and *she was lost. She hadn't heard or seen anything and had eventually stumbled out onto a road and had run along the roads for a long time searching for a trace of me or Sonny.*

When it had got dark she had kept on walking around, not knowing where she was, until eventually she had picked up my thought and used that as a point to navigate her way back to me. I felt that she had picked up my thoughts earlier in the day, too, but by the time she had run to me I had driven off.

Now some may say I have a fertile imagination, but I was in a forest of high trees where I couldn't hear a chainsaw from less than 100 yards away. There was no moon and the car headlights wouldn't penetrate the trees. The roads were very winding, as they followed the easiest path through rough terrain, so the headlights didn't reach far ahead. In any case, Bess approached us from behind, so she couldn't have seen the full beam. I'd switched off the car engine and the lights 30 minutes before she found us, so as far as I'm concerned she found us via telepathy.

I've had other experiences to back this up, but none so dramatic.

I'm with Roy on this one. The super senses of our animals are much more powerful than we know. Bess was attracted to the fear that Roy was emitting in the same way that Lord Byron kept his cool because I was letting him know I didn't want to pick a fight with a cheetah!

Sometimes, of course, animals just can't get their message across telepathically, so they have to try a more human level of communication. Step forward Charlie, who wasn't just a master of telepathy, but also a dog who knew how to get what he wanted!

We once left him with a dog sitter while we were on holiday and told her that he expected to be fed at 5 p.m. every day. She later told us that one evening she'd settled down to watch *Countdown* and sure enough, at 5 p.m. Charlie had appeared and let her know it was dinner time by sitting up on his hind legs and begging. She'd told him to wait a wee while until the show was over, and carried on watching. Suddenly the screen had gone blank, and she'd seen Charlie sitting there with the remote control in his mouth. Then he'd carried it through to the kitchen and dropped it into his food bowl! He was smart enough to use very human ways to get his message across, having sussed that lots of humans weren't very good at picking up telepathic clues. The dog sitter always fed him at 5 p.m. after that!

CHAPTER EIGHT

Animals, Spirit and Healing

How aware of spirit are animals? We've seen how they use their instincts to respond to their owners and to strangers, and how that's bound up in consciousness, but how alert are they to the more esoteric side of spirit, like ghosts, the presence of people who have passed, or to healing — occasions when there's a build-up of spirit energy?

The answer is that of course they're just as sensitive as a medium or anyone else who has allowed their spiritual side to develop. Not all animals are good at it, just as not all people are, but, as we've seen, they are more likely than a person to be alerted by a sense that's outside the five conventional ones — seeing, hearing, smelling, touching or tasting.

When I worked on *Most Haunted Live* in 2005 we did a four-day Halloween special in which the film crew, a team of mediums and a historian visited a series of sites in the East End of London. A German Shepherd called Max, who usually worked as a guard dog, joined us and that dog was onto spirit presence faster than any of the rest of the team!

While I was in the studio, the team visited the Blind Beggar pub in Whitechapel. Max went into a frenzy of barking and agitation at a certain spot in the bar where it turned out that the gangster George Cornell had been shot at point-blank range by Ronnie Kray in 1966. Now that dog can't read a newspaper, and I bet he's not a true-crimes expert, but he knew something terrible had happened there decades before.

It reminded me of something that happened with my old dog Cindy, whom the boys and I used to walk along a stream called the Luggy, a little way away from Cumbernauld. She loved the water and would go splashing and paddling after stones – she'd stick her head right under and root around to find a particular rock and nearly drown herself in the process!

We always came to a little bridge at one point on the walk and at the other end of it you could see what looked like a tunnel, with a small patch of sky at the far end. I once chucked a stone into the tunnel for Cindy and watched her bound after it, but just as she got to the entrance she slammed on the brakes and started yelping.

She'd frozen rigid with shock. Thinking she'd hurt herself, I hauled her out by her collar to check her paws, but she was fine. After a minute or so she was her old self again and I forgot all about it.

A week or two later I was walking her down by the stream again with Paul and Steven. Steven wanted to explore the tunnel, so we both waded into the water, leaving Paul on the bank reading a book. Cindy jumped after us. We got to the mouth of the tunnel and she froze again, then started to shake and whimper. Steven and I looked at each other and he said, 'Dad, can you feel anything? What's going on?'

I had a vague sense of something sinister, but no more than that, even though Cindy was now howling. I couldn't sense anything like a ghost, but that dog was picking up something that told her not to take another step.

We had to change our route on the way home to avoid passing the spot, though Cindy recovered quickly enough. I did wonder what had happened there, but I never went back to tune myself in properly – whatever it was, I didn't need to experience it. Cindy's warning was enough.

Like Max, I think she was reacting to a ghost, and a ghost isn't a spirit as such but a kind of stain or memory of an acute emotion – in the East End pub it was the fear and horror generated by the horrific murder of a violent man, and who knows what had happened in that tunnel. People will go to places which have these 'memories' without picking up anything untoward, but an animal will pull away and show pure fear as they feel that emotion go through them – and they won't blame it on 'a draught in the room'!

When you're talking about animals and the presence of spirit – not 'ghosts' – then of course it's true that they are fully aware of its benevolence and the great feeling of calm or the energy it can bring. Sometimes before a circle people ask, 'Is it OK for the cat to stay?' Why not? It might pick up on your unease, but if you're relaxed the animal will be relaxed too and will pick up on spiritual changes in the atmosphere – and they don't doubt them once they recognize them.

At one of my first sessions with a trance medium I learned that the animals participating were every bit as important as the humans taking part.

At the time Jim and I were living in a high-rise block of flats with fat old Elsa, who'd just had an operation on her hips and had to be practically carried about everywhere. We'd invited a very experienced medium called Laura to give a demonstration and were all sitting round, really excited about what we were going to see.

Laura went into her trance and we waited. Nothing happened. We carried on waiting, but there was no sign of any spirit coming through and Jim and I began to feel disappointed. Was this it? Was anything going to happen at all? Silence. And then, eventually, Laura spoke and brought through a spirit guide. Our joy was short-lived, though, because he said that he wouldn't work because the dog – he called her 'Four Legs' – wasn't comfortable. 'Everyone in this room needs to be content and settled,' he said, 'and then we will begin this teaching session.'

'Why isn't she comfortable?' we asked, looking at Elsa lying by the sofa and wondering what deep spiritual issues could be plaguing her.

'She needs to go to the toilet,' he replied, in a very down-to-earth fashion!

It was true – poor Elsa was dependent on us to take her down in the lift every few hours so she could relieve herself and in our excitement and greed to find out more from the spirit guide, we'd completely forgotten.

So we halted the session for a while and gave Elsa a chance to pee and then, with everyone in the room sitting comfortably, we began all over again and Elsa dozed off happily.

When you work with a medium, especially a trance medium, the level of energy in the room will change and every living being present has to be comfortable with that. This incident taught me that any time we wanted to practise this ourselves, we had to consult the part of everyone, animal and human, that was already functioning in the spirit world – and not forget their basic needs!

Many of the mediums and healers I've known over the years who've run their own private circles have kept animals who have joined in. I knew a medium in Spain who did trance work and he had two mynah birds who would fall absolutely silent when he worked. Wild birds would be drawn in too, landing on the windowsill and looking into the room.

The animals seldom get frightened, although sometimes they pick up on the arrival of a spirit and show that by becoming sensitive as well – so they develop their own ability to read the finer energies and atmosphere. Sometimes they read it better than the human mediums!

There was one occasion when we were doing a healing for a friend in the circle and Elsa wouldn't settle, which was very unlike her. She was so heavy that it was an effort for her to get up at all, so this was very unusual. We were trying to channel healing energy and direct it to the mother of a family I knew in Glasgow, as she was dying. It was a Sunday night and Dronma was with us, sketching away. All of a sudden Elsa, who'd been pacing around, started to cry, really whine, in a disturbing way. Soon none of us could meditate any more and we all sat in silence for a moment and watched her and thought, 'What is up with her? What is she trying to tell us?' The only person who was still active was Dronma, who carried on drawing. The doorbell rang, but the rule during the sessions was that nobody answered the door or the phone (which was unplugged), so nobody moved. Whoever it was gave up and went away.

We decided we couldn't do any more, so we closed the circle and Elsa stopped whining and settled down straight away. She just plopped down on the floor and went on being Elsa. We were having a cup of tea and chatting – 'What was that about? Something wasn't right tonight' – and Dronma said, 'Well, this is what I drew,' and showed us a sketch of a woman in a coffin wearing a cameo brooch. She looked very familiar.

We plugged the phone back in and there was an answerphone message from the woman whose mother we'd been praying for, saying that her mother had passed and she'd come round to ask us to pray for her, not realizing when she rang the doorbell that that's what we were doing. It turned out that Dronma had a little message from the mother to pass on, so I put her on the phone to the daughter.

As we all talked more, I also realized that Elsa hadn't been the only one who had been feeling uncomfortable. But she'd been the only sitter in the circle who'd known what that feeling meant and acknowledged it. The rest of us had just closed our eyes even more tightly and hoped that the feeling would go away. Usually if someone passed during a healing circle, everyone would come out of their meditation with a snap, but we needed Elsa to make us admit it that time.

Later on, when Jim and I moved to the Spiritualist church's basement and got Charlie, I started going to a lot of development meetings on Sunday nights in the church upstairs and honing my craft as a medium. I didn't want to take Charlie along, as I thought he'd race around being disruptive and then eat the sandwiches in the kitchen when we were meditating, so I'd leave him downstairs in the flat. He knew we were up there, though, and he'd cry and paw at the door, so in the end I decided to let him join in.

I couldn't have been more surprised by his behaviour. Cheeky Charlie was a different dog. This was where we saw the gentle side of him win out. No barking, no running about – he was just calm and thoughtful, almost as though he were joining in himself. He soon became a part of the sessions in his own way. As we sat round in the circle and began to try and tune out the outside world, Charlie would make his way round us all, one at a time, resting his chin on each of us as though he was counting us into an altered state of consciousness before moving on to our neighbour. He always went the same way round, to my left, and never skipped a person. Then he'd go to sleep on my feet while we meditated. He never shattered the calm or broke our meditations.

When the leader calmly ended the session, Charlie would go back round the circle, putting his chin on each person's lap until they opened their eyes. Then he'd wait patiently while we all recounted our experiences and Dronma showed her sketches. Finally, when everyone had finished, he would wag his tail and start woofing and jumping up at everyone – probably thinking about the sandwiches and acting like a dog all over again. He really understood what was going on and he was part of the circle for six years. Everyone knew him and loved him. I tried to do the same with young Meg, but that only lasted one go – she went leaping round the room with her tail going, jumping into everyone's lap, licking their face and generally being a total springer spaniel.

At the end of a circle we humans would sit around and chew the fat, trying to work over the finer points of the evening, but Charlie and Elsa would just want food. And they were quite right to do so – it was over! Back to the everyday! Why question or doubt or try to expand on your experiences? You'll only wind up downplaying something that really happened or else create a scenario that never happened. That's not living in the moment and learning your lessons.

There were only two occasions when Charlie disrupted a circle. Once he very gently woke us all up early with his usual procedure. As we were all sitting around looking at each other and wondering why he'd done that, the doorbell rang. Charlie must have known someone was coming and hadn't wanted us to be rudely interrupted.

The other occasion was a different kettle of fish. A group from outside the church had hired the hall to conduct what they grandly called a séance. I'd gone out for the night and my son Steven was at home in the basement flat with Charlie, so I told him that whatever happened, he mustn't let Charlie escape. I had to dodge round the door to get out without Charlie squeezing after me and I left him sitting behind the door on the top stair, his ears pricked and his face desperate – he knew there was a meeting going on in the church and he wanted to join in.

Steven told me what happened later, as did some friends of mine who had decided to sit in on this séance and see what the visiting mediums were up to. Down in the flat Steven was trying to watch the telly and calling to Charlie to settle down. The doorbell rang and Steven went upstairs to the door and said, 'Move, Charlie,' pushing him back a little. He opened the door and Charlie wriggled right under it and went racing down the hall, heading for the church. Steven went running after him but he couldn't catch the springer. Charlie hit the church door at full speed, barking at the top of his lungs, *whomp!*

In the hall the medium had been busy creating a spooky atmosphere with lots of wailing and theatrics to get everyone in the mood – he was doing everything but making the chairs levitate and having rapping on the table – and then in launched this spaniel bomb, barking and barking at him, 'Woof! Woof! Woof!' That was it – the séance was over. The medium was furious and started saying Charlie was possessed by an 'evil spirit' – that's a joke! My friends later told me Charlie's appearance was the best thing that happened all evening. It's funny that he knew these guys weren't legit – it was common to have visiting mediums at the church who were complete strangers and Charlie never gave them any hassle. But he barked like that when he was frightened or disturbed, so he obviously sensed these characters were up to no good.

Healing also naturally draws animals to take part. One healer, Sue Johnson from Surrey, England, has experienced a helping paw from a furry friend:

I am a healer and have held meditation groups in my home. One evening a friend of mine was sitting in a chair in my living room and she was feeling very low, as her own cat had recently died and she was missing him dreadfully. It was the height of summer and my cat Moppet came in through the open window, sat next to her and very gently reached out and placed his paw on her lap. He doesn't often go to other people, but he wanted to sit next to her. My friend broke down in tears.

If I'm conducting a healing, Moppet will bang on the door and try to sneak into the room and sit under the therapy table. He'll sit right next to me and purr very loudly. He does the same when I meditate – he'll fight to get as close to me as possible!

Maybe it's the atmosphere of calm that draws the animals in, but it would be wrong to say that they don't understand what's going on. I've seen too many animals respond to a healer's hands. I'll see someone's pet dog and the owner will say, 'Poor thing has a stomach ache,' and if I put my hand out to it, I know it'll move itself so my hand is over the painful part. Sometimes it'll even push its body up under my hand. Animals will let you know where the problem is.

Old Elsa had bad hips and she'd had a few operations on them. Whenever I had a friend round who was a healer, Elsa would reverse into them, hips first, as they sat on the sofa. They'd always remark, 'This dog puts herself up for healing.' And it was true – Elsa knew exactly what she wanted! Animals can definitely register and understand healing.

Charlie liked to lie on my feet and sit patiently throughout a healing, but as a dog who took on a lot of karma in his life, on more than one occasion he ended up being the patient himself.

One day Jim's sisters begged to be allowed to take Charlie out for a walk. We tried to put them off by pointing out that he was a real handful and that he'd just run all over the place and wouldn't come when they called, but they swore they'd be fine, so they took him off to the park. They hadn't been out for long, though, when he disappeared. At first they were annoyed, but when they'd been calling for him for ages and he still hadn't burst out of the bushes with a big grin on his face, they began to get worried.

Suddenly they heard him yelping in the distance, and ran in the direction of the noise. There was a little railing in front of a steep slope that led into a gorge with a stream at the bottom. There was Charlie, halfway down the slope and pinned to the ground. He must have leapt over the railing and chased down to the stream, hoping for a swim. It was so steep that the girls couldn't get down to him, but a passer-by heard their distress and climbed over and edged down the bank to Charlie. He had somehow caught himself under a root or branch which was sticking out of the earth and digging into his chest at the shoulder joint. He must have slid right under it and got snagged on it. The passer-by eased him free and carried him back up to the girls, who were beside themselves. They took him between them, though he was quite a heavy dog, and brought him back home to us, sobbing and full of apologies. They thought he was going to die.

Jim and I popped Charlie straight into the car and took him to the vet. A huge lump had come up in his shoulder. The vet felt him over and said, 'This doesn't look good. I'm going to need to do a biopsy. Bring him back tomorrow, but have a think tonight – this might be serious.'

Back home I phoned all the healers I knew to tell them I needed their help for Charlie, and of course they all agreed to send thoughts. I sat up all night with him, healing him. Eventually I went to bed and left him in his basket.

In the morning Charlie was transformed. He was up and running around grinning, not sick or in pain. I took him to the vet's to get the all-clear, just in case. He checked Charlie's shoulder again and looked dumbfounded. 'There's nothing there. The lump has gone, and his shoulder is fine.' He scratched his head and said he had no explanation for it. I had all the explanation I needed – that dog had had a healing and had responded to it. It wasn't the first time it had happened in his life and he had known what was going on and had let it happen.

What I didn't realize till much later was that every time Charlie was ill and I sent word out to the healers I knew, they told people at their local Spiritualist church, who would ask the congregation to send healing thoughts his way too. I only found out much later when I visited the churches and people asked after my dog, saying they'd been thinking of him for weeks. He was a very well-healed dog!

There have been all sorts of scientific experiments that have concluded that you have to have faith to be healed, but I know that's rubbish. How can an animal have faith? I don't believe Charlie or Elsa had a complex belief system, but they both had instinct, and that's how they responded. Healing is the natural process of one person or being having good intentions and wanting to help another being, and animals respond to positive emotions.

When Charlie was about eight and we'd just got Meg, we took them for a walk in the park. We were throwing tennis balls and sticks for them and they were chasing off after them, when they did Charlie's usual trick and vanished. We walked on, because we knew they'd come back soon enough, but when they reappeared Charlie was dragging his back leg and struggling to keep up with Meg. When he reached us, he couldn't even lift his head up to greet us or get his front paw up to show us he was hurt. There was no clue as to what had happened when they were out of sight – maybe he'd fallen awkwardly or run into something. Carefully, Jim and I picked him up and got him into the car with Meg.

When we were home he seemed OK, then suddenly he couldn't lift his head again. I ran my hands over him to try and see where the problem was, but he collapsed, so we took him to the vet, who gave him a quick check and sent us on to the animal hospital, where they had a scanner. By this point Charlie's back legs were failing and Jim and I were terrified. He'd been running around only a short time before and now it was as though his whole body was breaking down.

The hospital found a neurologist, who looked at the scan results and gave the poor spaniel the once-over. 'We think he's severed his spine,' she told us. 'It's rare, but it tends to happen more often in spaniels than other breeds. We can operate, but I've no idea if it'll work. He might never walk again, and you know what that means.'

When she said he'd broken his spine it was as though we'd been told he'd been sentenced to death. It's hard to imagine any animal or human surviving such a serious injury without being paralysed. Charlie hadn't been insured since his little stone-eating incident, so it was going to cost us. I'd just had a cheque for some royalties and it only just covered it, but we didn't hesitate and told her to go ahead. What else could we do? This was Charlie.

We had to give him another chance. He looked so miserable lying in the hospital. I gave him a stroke and whispered in his ear, and then we had to leave him there.

We went to see him the next day and he didn't look very good. He'd lost control of all his bodily functions and was hooked up to a catheter, which they said would probably only be temporary if he pulled through, but that felt like a big 'if'. He couldn't walk and two nurses had to carry him in a sling so that he could lie outside in the garden. It was awful to see. They told us that he'd take a few weeks to recover, if he was going to recover, and we made a fuss of him, then left.

We weren't allowed to see him for two weeks and when we were given permission to visit, Charlie didn't seem to be improving. He was off the catheter, but he still had to be carried out in the sling to pee outside and lie on the grass; he couldn't even lift his head to take a treat. The vets were trying to prepare us for the worst and I knew we'd have to let him go. It just wasn't fair on him – he'd loved to run and to chase things with Meg, and now here he was, a pathetic wee scrap having to be carried about in a sling.

Dronma called me and I told her the bad news. She listened and then said, 'You know, I've got some Tibetan medicine that a yogi gave me for my grandson. I don't know what's in it, but it's been prayed over by him. Give it to Charlie, and if he wants to live, he will, and if he wants to let go, he'll die. It's up to him to choose. Keep him another day and give him the medicine.'

I wasn't so sure, because it seemed unfair to keep Charlie alive in that state, but I decided to give it a go. Dronma brought me the medicine, which looked like an Oxo cube, and I set off to the hospital. Normally Tibetan medicine is something you wear in an amulet round your neck, but in really dire need you eat it.

Charlie had lost his appetite, so I didn't know if he'd take it. I wrapped it in a chew and held it to his mouth. He took it very feebly and I patted him as he swallowed it. I sat with him for 10 or 15 minutes, then helped the nurses take him outside to lie on the grass for a while. It was enough to break your heart. Leaving poor Charlie behind in hospital that night, I felt desperate.

Next day the phone rang at 7 a.m., when I was still asleep. I picked it up and tried to make out who was phoning me at that time of the morning – it was difficult because she was in tears. Eventually she calmed down enough to speak properly and I realized it was one of the nurses at the animal hospital. 'What's happened?' I asked her.

'Oh,' she said, 'it's amazing! Charlie was up this morning. He was on his feet and he went outside for a pee and we didn't need the sling at all.'

'What?'

'You can come and take him home now – I can't believe it.'

I got dressed quickly and headed over to the hospital, and sure enough there was Charlie, on his feet, even wagging his tail a little. The neurologist advised me to take him to a hydropool for swimming a few times because he was very weak after nearly a month of being unable to move, so I bundled him up in the car and took him home for a long recuperation.

We had to be very patient. He crumpled up when we got home and it wasn't till the next day that he was back up on his feet and walking around. We had to take him swimming one day, then let him recover the next, then take him swimming again the day after. He was exhausted each time and we'd watch him stumble and his legs fail him and we'd be terrified that he was permanently paralysed after all. He'd lost not only muscle but also body memory – he'd totally forgotten how to walk and run. It took him two weeks to get back to strength and be running around with Meg once more.

The only thing that changed permanently was his back legs. One day I was watching him and Meg romping through the bracken on a hillside when I realized there was something funny about the way he was bounding along. His back legs were moving together like a rabbit's – his front legs were normal but the rest was a bunny hop.

⌒

CHAPTER NINE

Messages from
the Other Side

When I was working on the documentary about pets in the afterlife, the producer asked if I would give a reading to a young woman who was also in the programme, and of course I said yes. They told me an edited version of the reading was to be included in the film.

We were filming near a pet cemetery which was up on a hillside in Perthshire with breathtaking views. You couldn't have asked for a more scenic resting place. The TV people introduced me to Carole Macpherson, a lovely, shy girl with a short punky hairstyle, and I took her hand for a second to see if there was a message for her from the other side. I warned her that I wasn't sure if it would work, but I quickly picked up a sense of tremendous sadness. This young woman was deeply depressed.

'Immediately I take your hand I feel the depth of what you're going through,' I told her. 'It's such a sadness that I would say you actually wanted to leave this world at one point.'

Carole nodded.

'You're so down and so disconnected, and it's obvious you've lost an animal, but let me see if I can tune in.'

I quickly got a sense of a wee Yorkie and I saw her jumping up at Carole.

'She's a little girl, isn't she? A Yorkshire terrier? I can see her jumping onto your lap. She's got another Yorkie with her too. She's a really bouncy dog, keeps leaping up and kissing me. She's got fabulous ears – I don't know why I have to say that, but her ears are her feature.'

Carole smiled and said yes, that was her dog. She was buried next to another little terrier of the same breed, so that must have been the other dog I saw.

Then the dog showed me what had happened to her. 'She's bleeding from her rear end – it was kidney problems and that's why you had to put her to sleep.'

Carole accepted this, saying that was exactly what had happened.

'It takes a lot of bravery to put a dog to sleep when you love them and you've really connected to them in this life. Have you been thinking of joining the dog?'

Carole suddenly said, 'Yes, I have. She's been the only thing I've felt love for in 10 years.'

I realized how awful it had been for her, but the dog had more to show her mistress.

'There must be a picture of her wearing clothes somewhere.

I know this is going to sound funny, but there is, isn't there?'

Carole got the giggles and looked at the crew, who were all grinning away. I didn't know that earlier they'd filmed her treasured photos of the dog dressed up in a little jumper.

When the cameras stopped rolling I learned more about Carole's story. When the dog had passed she'd used up what little money she had getting her a plot in the pet cemetery. She'd only been 18 when she'd had to make the decision to let the dog go and it was the hardest choice she'd made in her life. The dog had been her best friend and afterwards she'd been in so much emotional pain that she had started to self-harm.

She'd told the documentary makers, 'When I lost her, I wanted to run across the Taymore bridge and jump in. I'd do anything to be with her.'

In the two years since, she'd visited the grave twice a week without fail, and she liked to sit and talk to the dog because she sensed that she could hear what she was saying. She'd placed a little toy windmill by the headstone with the flowers and said that on some still days the windmill would suddenly start spinning, which she saw as a sign that the Yorkie was able to hear her.

'Maybe people think I'm mad, but it's my way of thinking,' she said, and I think she was right to see it that way.

I asked her, 'Can you remember how your dog reacted when you were happy and loved her?'

'Yeah, she was all over me, jumping up and kissing me, the happiest little thing in the world.'

'And can you remember how she behaved when you were sad?'

'She used to go and sit in a corner and not communicate with me and then I'd feel guilty because I'd pushed her away from me.'

'Well, think of the sadness you're feeling at the moment. That's what you're doing to your dog in the spirit world. You're not comforting her by mourning her, you're keeping her away from you. The love that you've built up doesn't die. And that animal will never leave your side. Even spiritually she'll never ever leave your side. That dog's not in the grave, she's with you everywhere. She's a sassy wee lassie, isn't she?'

By this point Carole was like a new girl – her whole face had changed and you could tell she felt a real connection with the dog for the first time since her death. 'Her name was Sassy,' she said. 'She even had a T-shirt with it written on the front!'

I was glad to be able to help Carole come to terms with her loss and reconnect with Sassy, who I'm sure is as capable of making her presence felt now as she was in life! She came back with a message for Carole for the same reason that many human spirits communicate with their loved ones – she saw that she was struggling and low and she wanted to help her and to raise her up. The case is a reminder of how difficult it is for us when we have to take the responsibility of letting our beloved pets go. Carole was distraught, but she made the right decision, and Sassy showed that love can get through anything when it has to.

The way animals choose to communicate can tell us a lot about their personality in life. Vicky's husband Bob felt his pet goat Stella brushing into him and demanding his attention, and she also had an eye for her dinner dish! Sally Foster of Ipswich, in England, had a dog I like the sound of, whom I'll call Mystic Megan:

> I had my very beautiful white German Shepherd Megan for nine years. We were constant companions, and after she died in July 2005 one of her toys, a duck, used to start quacking without rhyme or reason. At first it freaked me out and my husband thought I was cracking up, then one day it happened in front of him! I feel sure it was Megan's way of getting in touch.

My friend Jan Brook, who's also a medium, brought through an unusual character when she was doing a demonstration in front of a whole churchful of people. She had just finished bringing one message through when she was suddenly aware of a monkey – a monkey in uniform, no less – who got closer and closer until it was virtually sitting on her shoulder. It was dressed in scaled-down army khakis. She turned to the audience and said, 'Well, I don't know how to say this, but a monkey's just come through and I've no idea how to communicate with it.'

That's when the monkey lit a cigarette and started to blow smoke rings! Straightaway Jan got the sense of this little fellow's personality – so laid-back he was practically horizontal. He puffed away, then picked up a pint of beer and began to drink it. She told everyone what was happening and just about brought the house down, and a lady stood up to claim the reading. It turned out that the monkey had belonged to her grandfather when he had been fighting in North Africa during the Second World War, and he'd been a kind of regimental mascot. The soldiers had taught him to blow smoke rings and to sip his beer with the best of them. The woman had never met the monkey herself, but her grandfather had told her plenty of stories about him; in fact, in her handbag that night she had a photo of him with the monkey. After that, her granddad came through in person and brought her a message, although I bet Jan wasn't the only one who wondered what the monkey himself might have had to say!

Albert Best once told me he watched the great Scottish medium Helen Duncan materialize an elephant to an audience of 30 or 40 people in Glasgow, and the elephant's form suddenly shaped itself out of a white cloud of ectoplasm. She didn't just bring it through to show off, though – there was a genuine connection between the animal and one of the sitters in the séance. Albert believed that Helen's spirit guides allowed the phenomenon to occur to show those present that all types of being can come back to us from spirit if we have loved them in this life. He also told me how stunning it was to witness, although no one was more bowled over than the man who had actually tended and cared for this animal in

Africa some years earlier. They say elephants never forget – how true in this case!

When I look back at all the readings I've given when a cherished pet came through, I think the ones that have struck me most have had nothing to do with the exotic type of the animal or the tricks they could do, and everything to do with the force of personality the communicator could show, and the wave of warmth that they brought with them.

I was giving a reading in Austria earlier this year to a couple through a translator, and their little son came through. I sensed that the child, Marcus, had had some kind of disability or chronic condition in life and that it had eventually killed him. He had only been four and a half, and I understood that that was as long as he had been expected to live. He told me that he was fine and everything was good and that he wanted to thank his parents.

They were very moved, but it was the next sign he gave that brought them to tears of joy. He showed me a white English bull terrier running around in a circle, chasing its tail and then stopping and panting away with its tongue hanging out of its mouth, and a little awkwardly the boy wrapped his arms round its neck and the dog put his face to the boy's face and gave his ears a good licking. The laughter that came out of that little boy then was the most magical I've ever known, and that's when I heard the name 'Snoopy'.

When I told the parents, they were amazed and delighted, and more so when Marcus said that Stefan was there too.

The mother said, 'That's my other son. I'm so glad they're all together and they've got Snoopy.' The translator was almost crying too much to pass on the message. The mother told me that when Marcus had been alive the most uplifting experience he'd had was when Snoopy had licked him, and the dog had only to walk into the room and he'd start smiling and giggling that knockout giggle. He'd loved to see the dog chase its tail, and it had often seemed that Snoopy had done it purely to entertain him. Marcus's hand had been deformed, which was why it had been difficult for him to hug the dog, but that hadn't stopped him.

The image of the dog chasing its tail was so important to the message — that set the seal on it, showing the parents the happiness their sons could still experience on the other side.

Lots of people say it must be hard to take a message from an animal because they don't speak, but in cases like Snoopy's it's just not a problem. It's pure feeling, perfect memories from the jewel box, a direct projection of happiness that's like a shot in the arm. Who could do that better than a dog?

Animals are no different from people. Some are animated; some are not. There are a lot of people who are very bland and it's actually difficult as a medium to say anything about them. I've lost count of the number of people to whom I've had to say, 'I've got your husband here and he's not talking a lot,' and then they've laughed and told me that's exactly how he was in life. The animals in this book, though, are all stand-outs, really extraordinary personalities.

One of the most outstanding animal communicators I've ever known took his bow when I was writing this book and on tour in South Africa, in April 2008. I was presenting an evening of mediumship at a theatre in Johannesburg when a Bruno came through and started running around madly. I thought at first he was a person – after all, spirits have done stranger things in readings I've given – so I just went on telling the audience what I was sensing and then suddenly I froze and blurted out, 'Oh, my God! It's a dog!' And there he was: a grey and white Staffy with strange blue eyes.

A man in the auditorium called Robin raised his hand and said that Bruno was his dog and he'd had to have him put to sleep just the week before. When he spoke, the Staffy ran round in circles like mad. I said, 'He has someone here with him and it's a woman. Her life was taken by somebody else, but Bruno is bringing her through and he's happy that he's got her with him.'

It was Robin's sister. She'd been murdered in a carjacking only a short time before, so he'd lost both her and the dog in the space of a few weeks. What made this an extraordinary reading was the fact that I'd never come across an animal that was such a communicator. It was the most detailed and accurate message I've ever passed on from a dog, complete with names, addresses and dates. Bruno even showed me where the girl was murdered, of all things, although he had never been there.

I told his owner, 'This is crazy, but this dog can really get his message across! He's showing me all sorts of things about your sister's death.'

Robin said, 'If you knew Bruno, you'd know why. He communicated with people every day, especially my sister, and it always sounded as though he was trying to make words. This is no surprise to me!'

I sensed Bruno leaping between Robin in the audience and the woman to the left of him, all four feet off the floor, like a lamb. Robin explained that this was his other sister and that Bruno used to jump like that whenever she came into the house.

Later he told me that Bruno had been a 'very discerning dog' and only chosen very special people to love. He'd absolutely adored the young lady who'd died. I just got the feeling that Bruno had gone into the spirit world to protect her and look after her. Robin showed me a photo of the Staffy and there he was, personality bursting out of the picture.

I'm pretty sure Bruno wouldn't have needed me to come through and communicate with his family, but the circumstances were right and he made sure he was there for his starring role — I think he liked a bit of fame and fortune, and I'm sure he wanted to be in this book.

The next two stories are about animals who found other ways of proving they were still with their families after death, with no help from mediums. Astrid Wareham from Cape Town in South Africa, the woman who adopted Redge, told me another story about a special cat:

Jethro came from my husband's family. One of his aunts kept cats and Jethro came from one of their litters. She was a blue-eyed silvery tabby cross Siamese. When she was eight weeks old she somehow fell into the pond in their back garden and almost drowned. My husband's uncle fished her out and resuscitated her as best he could, but she was always a little strange after that and we thought it was perhaps because she'd been brain-damaged through oxygen deprivation.

She was lovely company, though, larger than life, and like lots of Siamese she was very talkative. If I sang a song like 'Happy Birthday' and left out a word, she'd fill in the blanks with a 'meow'. She always wanted to know what was going on and who was in the house, and guests would ask, 'Where's Jethro tonight?' If I was feeling blue, she'd always climb onto my lap and offer some comfort – every time. She liked to snuggle up to me and suck on my jersey as though she were suckling, and if I was standing in the kitchen peeling potatoes she'd jump up and grab my back pockets, then climb up to sit on my shoulder.

She was such a busybody that I had to be careful how I left the house if I was going for a long walk, because she'd follow me if I didn't lock her in. Once I was driving down the road when our neighbours, who were driving in the opposite direction, flagged me down. They were laughing so hard that all they could do was point at the roof of my car, and when I looked up, there was Jethro, curled up in a ball and enjoying the ride!

We'd had Jethro for six years when one spring morning I felt a sudden grip across my heart and sensed that my little cat was going to pass soon. I whispered in her ear that she didn't have permission to leave us – I couldn't face the thought of losing her. But a few weeks later the awful news came – Jethro had been knocked down by a car on the road outside our house and killed. We held a little funeral service for her and buried her in a corner of the garden.

That night I dreamed that I was standing in my lounge when Jethro came walking in from the garden. I was so relieved to see that she was OK, but my rational mind couldn't accept that the cat we had buried was now fine and strolling into the house. I was about to scoop her up into my arms and hug her when that rational mind took over and the dream ended.

For several days after her death my daughter and I would see Jethro sleeping in her favourite spots around the house. We would instantly recognize her and then the image would vanish. Since then I've also had the odd dream where Jethro and I have snuggled together like old times.

I believe she stayed with us while we were mourning her – something she chose to do to ease our pain.

If Jethro eased her owner's pain in life when she was feeling blue, then it makes perfect sense that she would be drawn to her grief and help to make it subside. What a lovely little cat.

Lindsey Wingate of Buckinghamshire, England, also found an unforgettable friend when she went looking for a new addition to her family:

I wanted to buy an English mastiff pup as a companion for our Great Dane, Stanley, and when I visited a breeder one of the little puppies just stood out to me and I chose him. We called him Barney. The two dogs were very, very close and devoted to me and my young children. Both of them were amazing, very 'different' dogs.

Stanley saved me from a nasty accident one day by barging me into a wall. I was just telling him off when a lorry came careering past with one wheel up on the pavement – it would have hit us if he hadn't shoved me out of the way. He sensed things about people, too, and I learned to listen to him. If he thought someone was a threat he would go very quiet and still, and though you couldn't hear his growl I could feel it and see his eyes fixing on that person.

Our neighbour had threatened my life and those of my family and was violent to his own children and wife, and though Stanley had never seen any of that he would start up his warning bark whenever this nasty man passed our house on the street. He also loved to lie under my feet when I was meditating or channelling spirit in the garden.

Barney had an old soul; he never did puppy nips or jumping up and was always sensitive towards everyone, as a good older dog is. He was just happy to be with people, including my young kids, one of whom was only months old.

Our local vet found that Barney had a heart murmur and we planned to take him to a London veterinary hospital for a fuller examination. I was to go with my husband and the baby, but on the day I saw my husband stride past in a suit holding Barney's lead. I asked him to wait and he said he was not going to take me and the baby (then recovering from surgery) along after all. There was no telling him any different and so I held Barney's head and kissed him and told him to be good.

The next news came much later that day. Barney had been euthanized and my husband had felt it wasn't worth telling me beforehand. I was heartbroken, though I agreed that it was for Barney's sake, as all four valves of his heart were broken, but I was angry not to have been consulted or informed. I actually did not speak to my husband for two or three days because I was so angry.

That night I sat outside as the sun set, having a cigarette. The dogs' beds were out in the garden and Stanley was lying on his with his head on Barney's bed. They'd moved their beds close to each other so they could be together. Stanley was sniffing at the scent of Barney on the cushion and crying a bit, and wouldn't come to me when I called him. I knew he was grieving.

Then through my own tears I saw a shape at the end of the garden — and realized it was Barney, walking slowly up the path and looking at me in that sweet sad way of his. I cried tears of beauty just looking at him and then he faded. When I looked at Stanley, I realized he'd seen Barney too. He was staring at the place where Barney had been and then he came running over to slobber some comfort on me. Both of us were a bit emotional!

I got up to go indoors and make the tea and then I heard a strange sound. Stanley was running around the garden with the dog beds, one at a time, shaking them. He laid Barney's far away from his and then dragged his own into the house for the night. He knew Barney wasn't coming home.

My two youngest children were 18 months and three months old when Barney passed, but for the next two or three years every Christmas they played with a dog called Barney who liked to run all round the ground floor of the house. The kids told me the dog's name and what he looked like, even though they were both too young to remember us having him and we didn't have any photos. They're nine and eleven now and they still write letters to Barney, 'remembering' him.

Stanley died last year at the ripe old age of eleven and a half – most Great Danes only live to be eight – but both dogs have come back through mediums at church to say hello to me and my children.

My husband and I divorced eight years ago and my Spiritualism has seen me through long years as the single parent of five children. Now I'm doing a degree in social work and am ready for a new dog to choose us.

Why wouldn't an animal like Barney come back to the people he loved and shared a life with? People come back to protect and guide us, and these animals loved us in the same way, so they are there to be our protectors and comforters in spirit as they were in life. They just go on doing that.

The only problem people have with the notion of animals coming back is their own limited minds. We think of ourselves as different from animals when we should be recognizing them as spirits, souls, at a level on which we can connect and become bonded. When we make that connection, then our mind is open enough.

Communication from an animal might not come through a dream or an apparition, just something as simple as a sudden sense of that pet. Then you have to work out why you thought of them and what they could be trying to tip you off about. That you need to look after yourself, perhaps? Or to wake up to something that's going on? That's what my first dog Lassie still does for me, decades after she passed.

In fact Lassie has become a kind of psychic early-warning system. When she appears in my dreams I know I have to pay attention to what's going on around me, because it almost always means that someone somewhere means me harm. Once I dreamed a wolf was attacking me, lunging at my neck, and Lassie appeared from nowhere and fought it off. Another time I was working in a situation that made me really uneasy, although I hadn't figured out why. During that time I had an incredibly vivid dream where I was walking, as I always am in these dreams, in the pheasant fields, following a path, when suddenly a snake reared up, a cobra. I knew it was going to strike me but, trapped in the dream, I didn't do anything but turn my back on it. The next thing I knew, Lassie ran up and jumped between me and the cobra as it lashed out. The snake's fangs struck Lassie and she fell to the ground. Then the snake disintegrated and Lassie just picked herself up, shook herself and was fine. And this sensation of being protected ran right through me. When I woke up, the strange feeling that there was something nasty out there waiting to strike me still lingered and it took me a few days to work out the meaning of the dream. Finally I realized someone was trying to trick me into getting in trouble so they could score some points, and I could see who they were and what they were up to. I got out of that place, thanking Lassie for the protection.

Now I don't know if that was actually Lassie in spirit or if it was just my mind sensing that something was wrong and producing the image of Lassie, but what I was left with was the sensation that someone was looking out for me and protecting me. Lassie is a very personal symbol of trust and friendship for me, so I know to pay attention to her when she makes an appearance.

I know that many people have had experiences of their animals returning to them after death, some with important messages or warnings, some to bring a feeling of comfort by showing that they are safe and free from any suffering or pain now. More than anything, though, they come back because they love us, and it's because they love us that they can.

CHAPTER TEN

~

Reincarnation?

If you start talking about animals living on after death, then sooner or later you'll come across some joker who starts making comments about 'past lives' and asking if your big old ginger cat is the reincarnation of Mary, Queen of Scots. My mum used to joke that Lassie was my granddad, but while they had a few things in common, I don't remember Granddad jumping into the river Kelvin to chase swans!

In *The Unbelievable Truth* I quoted the Dalai Lama: 'To understand the nature of rebirth, you first have to understand consciousness.' I compared consciousness to a computer hard drive which contains many 'programs' or lives; while only one of these programs might be running, the rest are stored in the memory and can be tapped into or might influence the life that's happening now.

If animals are, as we've seen, a part of the greater consciousness, then of course it follows that they too participate in reincarnation – they're programs on the hard drive too. But how do they take part? And how do you recognize it when it happens?

There are two ways in which animals fit into the grand cycle of reincarnation. These next two stories illustrate the first way perfectly. The first story comes from my friend Loretta, who had no difficulty accepting reincarnation when she saw it and walked alongside it:

Six months after I lost my brother Raz to cancer, my friend Leanne lost her husband Al to the same disease. We hadn't known each other all that well before, but after all we went through losing them together, we became very connected. We decided to go on a trekking tour in Bhutan in the Himalayas together; I had always wanted to go. We arranged to hike in a very remote part of the country and camp with a team of local guides – we were really getting away from civilization as we knew it.

On our first day out in the mountains a large black-and-white dog appeared and walked with us. The only wild animals up there were yaks and wild dogs, so we kept asking our guides, 'Whose is the dog?' And they replied that he had probably come from the local monastery and that when he wanted to he'd turn round and head home. After five hours, the dog was still at our side and we were worried he would get lost, but the guides assured us he would be fine.

The strange thing is, both Leanne and I found ourselves, separately, talking to this dog. As we climbed higher and higher the altitude thinned and it got harder to walk and breathe. I freaked out a little because there was so little oxygen that I was getting pins and needles. Leanne was struggling and fell behind, and the dog fell back with her.

When she walked, it walked; when she stopped, it stopped. She tried to follow one of the horsemen, but he walked too quickly and she lost him, which left her alone in the dark, apart from the dog. Still in his company, she caught up with the rest of us at the next camp, and she was quite emotional, wondering, 'I don't know what possessed me to follow a stray dog in the mountains.' We were both shocked by it.

We started to joke that the dog was my brother Raz and her husband Al come back to look after us, because it was obvious that was what he was doing. We called him Rally and he refused to sleep in our tiny tent out of the cold, keeping guard outside instead. He wouldn't take water or accept a blanket, although sometimes he took a little meat. We had to place the meat down and move away, as the dog would never let us stroke him or touch him; he wouldn't come close enough for us to try. He didn't seem to interact with any of the other animals, just shadowed our heels all day.

In the morning he stirred only when we did and by the time we'd packed he was by our side. He was just there for all five days. We kept worrying about him, in case he was too far from home, but the guides still said he would be fine.

Finally we reached the village where the road back to the town started, and this was the end of our trek. One of the villagers invited us in and then took us on a tour of the local school. When we came out, the dog was no longer there. No one saw him leave, even though we were in a huge open area and he would have been noticeable.

Our guides were devout Buddhists and there was no doubt in their minds that Rally was a protector guiding us. They understood perfectly.

I knew Gordon would pick up on this, so when I got back to the UK, even though I spoke to him on the phone a couple of times I didn't tell him anything. Then three weeks later I was out with Gordon and Jim for the evening and Jim asked me to tell him about the Himalayas. I said I'd had some very strange powerful spiritual experiences there and there was something I wanted to talk to Gordon about. Jim told me not to tell him anything but save it to tell Gordon later.

And guess what? Gordon did have a message for me. A week or two later he called up and said that when he'd been in the shower that morning he'd had a message from Raz: 'Tell my sister I was with her the whole time in the Himalayas. I guided her and protected her and showed myself to her as a dog, because I could.'

I was exceptionally close to my brother and it is just what he would have done. I had deliberately kept my story from Gordon so that if Raz had come through to confirm it, I'd know it was true.

Who's to say that dog even physically existed on that trip? I think he was probably just an emanation of the minds of the two men, Raz and Al, which reached Loretta and Leanne in the form of canine protection. And even though that dog wasn't a kind of snuggly pet, he emanated pure benevolence.

Sadly, in our human state we are governed by the limits put on our mind by logic and rationality. In some ways we need these guidelines so we can stay grounded in human reality, but even within that reality things can happen that defy everything we've been taught. We're only just beginning to understand that there are many levels to our consciousness.

Loretta and Leanne were in a highly spiritual place when they had their experience. Two worlds meet in the Himalayas, real magic can happen there and Loretta and Leanne both found themselves reaching a deeper state of awareness.

This next tale comes from Angela Latchford of Hertfordshire, England, and it's an even more incredible story of emanation by a truly extraordinary person.

When my father-in-law, Ronald, was a young man he had a little mongrel dog called Bess who used to accompany him up the road to the bus stop when he went to work and be there in the same spot to greet him in the evening when he came home. When he was called up to serve in the army (REME) in the Second World War, the little dog walked him to the end of the road, said goodbye and returned home.

That evening Bess didn't stir to go and wait for him, and she didn't go out to meet him again until he did return, nearly four years later. Somehow the dog knew exactly when he would return, even though Ron had been on the other side of the world for four years. When my daughter Alison was growing up, my father-in-law loved to tell her the story about the dog, and she always asked to hear it.

My father-in-law was a great man, a real character, always bright and bubbly. He had been a prisoner of war in the Far East for most of his four years away and afterwards he always felt he was living on borrowed time and had to make the most of his life. He had survived against the odds many times and knew he must have someone up there looking out for him. He had been shipwrecked not once but three times and been rescued once and swept to the shore twice, while others around him had been carried out to sea and never seen again. His worst experience had been on a prison ship where men were being dragged out of the hold dead or raving and, with them all deprived of rations, he had even watched his comrades drink their own urine to survive. That ship had been bombed by an American plane and when he had finally made it to another American ship with other soldiers, while sitting below deck the men on either side of him had been killed when that too had been machine-gunned. Later, he had been working as a forced labourer in a coal mine at Nagasaki and had come up to the surface one day to see the twisted metal of the mine's lifting gear in an otherwise barren wasteland with the atomic 'mushroom' cloud rising over the city.

When he retired he was very active with the other veterans of his regiment and started to write up his experiences, which I could barely bring myself to read, they were so horrific. He had so many horrendous tales to tell that I think it must have been his saving grace that he never bottled it all up and suffered in silence.

He also loved to paint, mainly submarines and ships, and he and Alison would sit down side by side and work together for hours. He would encourage her to paint and there they'd sit with a piece of paper each, sketching away. They were very close to each other and shared a real bond.

She had a real thing about dogs and always wanted one of her own, but our lifestyle meant we couldn't be tied to the home by a pet. In particular, she wanted a little white dog, so her grandfather used to bring her ornaments, brooches or toys whenever he went away to the seaside or elsewhere and they always featured a little West Highland white terrier.

When he was 78 years old, he was diagnosed with cancer and the doctors said there was a possibility that the fallout he had experienced near Nagasaki had led to it. He fought the disease for four years and I nursed him, along with my mother-in-law, Joyce, in his last days. As he lay there at home, he was half the size of the person he'd been and he'd lost all his hair due to the chemo. Even then, he was trying to look after us all, telling his wife how his funeral should be and how she should get us all away for a holiday when it was over.

During those last days, while lying in his bed, he regressed back to the PoW camps and several times I saw him slowly raise his hands, put them together and place them on his head just as the Japanese guards had made the prisoners do when they sat for hours in the sun. I'd tell him, 'It's all *right, Dad, you're not in the camps, you're at home,' and he'd lower his hands, only to repeat the action again a little later. Towards the end, he was trying to tell me something, but I couldn't understand what it was, and after he slipped away I felt very guilty about this and thought maybe he had wanted me to fetch his wife, who had been asleep upstairs. He was the first member of the family that we'd lost, and we were all devastated, especially Alison.*

At his funeral the Royal Naval Association turned out in force and a standard was placed on his coffin. None of us had realized just how well known he had been or that he had been respected like royalty by these people.

In the days following, when I was going through his things in the garage, I found a half-finished painting of a Westie holding a slipper in its mouth that he'd been working on for Alison.

Exactly one month after he had passed, we were all sitting in the living room watching the TV on a cold, damp evening when Alison went to the front door and came back looking puzzled to say there was a little white dog waiting outside. We went to see the dog and stroked her. She seemed very pleased to see us. Then we thought her owner was probably waiting for her somewhere and shooed her off. Later Alison glanced out of the window and said the dog was still on the drive. We went out again and made a fuss of her, then decided to walk her up and down the road looking for her owner, but there was no one in sight. We rang the police and the local dog warden, but no one had reported a lost pet. It was miserable outside, so we took her in overnight.

A week, then a month, went by and we were getting attached to the dog. We called her Sandie because she had a sandy stripe on her back and also because when she'd arrived we'd been watching Grease on the TV starring (of course) Olivia Newton John as Sandie. After three months we received a letter from the police saying we could legally claim her if we wanted to, and even though I'd never wanted a dog because I didn't want the mess, I said yes straightaway.

The vet told us that Sandie was between two and four years old and very small for her breed. She was the sweetest dog imaginable and so intelligent that she seemed almost human sometimes. Once when I was out in the garden clearing up her mess, I sighed and said, 'I wish you would do your business at the end of the garden,' and from that day on she did! It was extraordinary to think she'd understood.

She showed some other uncanny insights too. I was very good friends with a woman who'd been in hospital with me at the time that I was giving birth to my first daughter, Louise, and her son, Michael, had been very close to Alison when they were growing up. He was two years older than her and used to push her around in her baby walker when they were playing together. During her teenage years, he was her soulmate. He came to visit us one Sunday just before he went to university. He wasn't a dog lover, although Sandie liked him, but on this occasion she behaved very strangely. She clung to him, even sitting on his feet and refusing to let him move. I'd never known her do anything like that with anyone but my mother-in-law. Looking back, I wonder what she knew about that poor boy, because less than a week later he died in hospital of a brain haemorrhage that no one had predicted. He hadn't been sick or had any reason to believe he might suffer such a terrible blow, but it was as though Sandie knew something was wrong or had a premonition and wanted to comfort him.

The fact that my father-in-law had always known that Alison wanted a little white dog and Sandie had appeared so soon after his death made me wonder if he had sent the dog to help us get over his passing. It would have been just typical of him to find a way to ease Alison's grief. Gradually I began to realize that the Westie had more than a few things in common with that wonderful man. For a start, she loved my mother-in-law and paid her lots of attention. She would sit at her feet whenever she came to visit and never leave her side. She also liked to be in charge of the car. My father-in-law didn't like me, or indeed anyone, to drive him if he could drive himself or have my husband do it, and the first time I set out with Sandie on the passenger seat, she immediately climbed into my lap and put her paws up on the steering wheel as if to say, 'We're off now and I'm driving!' I pushed her away but she wriggled back into the same position again. In the end, I had to buy a restraint to keep her in her seat so I could drive in peace! I would always give in when we turned off the main road and were nearly home and would let her 'steer' us back. When we pulled up and I put the brake on, she'd always turn around and 'kiss' me on the nose. My husband had no such problems — she was quite happy to be just a passenger when he was in the driving seat, just as my father-in-law had been.

On the first Mothering Sunday following his death, the family was sitting around lazing after lunch when suddenly I saw a photo that was wedged into the frame of a mirror jump out and flip onto the coffee table more than a foot away. No windows were open and even if a freak draught had come through, the photo would have fallen directly onto the floor. Sandie watched all this and then looked at me as if to say, 'Did you see that?' The picture had landed face up and it was a photo of my husband's cousin Frances, who had been one of my father-in-law's favourite nieces. That must have been him letting us know he was there with us too.

We had Sandie for five years altogether, but after a year or so with us she started to show the symptoms of heart problems and had to have a pacemaker fitted. The strain of this gave her meningitis, which in turn left her with epileptic fits. She was looked after incredibly well by the Royal Veterinary College in Potters Bar and they admitted she'd survived something very few little dogs would have pulled through. Not so long after that she too was diagnosed with cancer and had to have chemotherapy every three weeks. It wasn't very aggressive, but it was a lot for her small body to cope with. I spent a lot of my time at home nursing her; I felt she was our connection to my father-in-law and I knew how much she meant to Alison.

I'd become interested in Gordon Smith's books because I was still feeling guilty about my father-in-law's last days and was wondering whether I had let him down or done the right thing. So I went along to see Gordon at a book signing and *talk at the local Civic Hall, Broxbourne, on 25 April 2007. The date was, by coincidence, my father-in-law's birthday. That evening I felt quite drawn to Gordon and strangely elated. I had a chance to meet him at the book signing afterwards but was so struck by a strong positive feeling that I would see him again soon that I handed my copy of the book over to the stage manager to get it signed on my behalf and left the building.*

Two days later the phone rang and it was a TV researcher from This Morning. I'd been so busy with Sandie that I'd completely forgotten that back in February or March I'd been watching the show when they had asked if any viewers would like a reading by a medium. You just had to send in a photo and a short note about yourself. It was unlike me to partake in anything like that and although I thought it was a strange thing to do, I walked over to the computer and e-mailed them a picture and said, 'My name is Angie and I would like a reading.' That was all. And now it turned out that I'd been chosen to see the mediums who would be on the show. I asked the researcher who they were, and she said that one of them was Gordon Smith! So I suppose it was meant to be.

Another lady and I went to the studios and the producers explained that neither of the mediums had been told anything about us, not even our names. We were even blindfolded so they couldn't pick up any visual clues. We were taken onto the set and I was placed with Gordon as the cameras started to film us. The moment Gordon took my hand, my whole body felt warm. He brought through my husband's nan and she really was there with us, then everyone came through, including my father, whom I'd recently lost. There was nothing ambiguous about it.

At one point Gordon even said, 'I'm getting "Latchford" – is that a name or a place?' and of course it was my surname. Everything he told me was factual and true. Then he said, 'There's a man here with smiling eyes singing "Angie, Baby",' and I knew it was my father-in-law, because he always used to sing that song to me. He gave me several pieces of evidence, then said that he knew about the apartment we'd just bought abroad – something he wouldn't have approved of when he was alive – and that he thought it was a good thing, but we had to check the small print. That was totally typical of him!

Finally he told me that we mustn't remember him when he was 'old and bald' but as he was in the photo we had of him going off to war, in his uniform and with all his hair. 'I'm here with the dog,' he said, and I knew that must be the little mongrel Bessie, who had waited so patiently for him to come back from the war. I think he must have known that I was still feeling worried about those last few hours and was letting me know that all was well and he was happy now. I was left feeling uplifted and relieved.

Sandie hung on with us for several more months and died just before Alison's twenty-second birthday, almost five years to the day after she'd first appeared on our doorstep. She was only a young dog, but in those five years she'd brought us so much comfort and joy and helped us cope with the loss of my

father-in-law, a dear loved one. I still miss her very much. She
brightened our lives and was a lovely little friend.

Maybe you could see this as straightforward reincarnation
– Ronald as a Westie! I think it's more likely, though, that
Ronald projected a small part of his consciousness into this
wee dog for a short time in order to help heal his family
and also stay connected to them in a loving way. The chain
of synchronicity here really is astounding – how did Sandie
know which doorstep to sit on, if she wasn't guided by
spirit?

Personality is a tiny thing compared to consciousness. When
you understand that you're limitless, the boundaries fall and
everything is possible.

And what about the second kind of reincarnation – when
an animal isn't just impressed with another person's
consciousness, but is actually a soul who has come back to this
plane in animal form? It's hard to find stories of this because so
much comes down to the owner's own impression – we can't
put a cat on the couch and give it a past-life regression! It may
also be something we never find out in this lifetime. I don't
know if I'll work out the full extent of how I was connected
to Charlie – that may take more lives to understand.

I do like this story from Angela Currie of Glasgow, though,
because it leads me on to the idea of 'soul groups'. She knew
a dog who acted as though he had a mysterious past life:

I grew up in Broomielaw in Glasgow in the seventies in a tenement building in the city centre, right next to the Clyde Port Authority. Our house and the one next door were the only ones that were occupied. My Auntie Alice lived there with her family and a mongrel called Whiskey, who was a right scabby-looking dog with a big black beard. He wasn't pretty to look at and we used to laugh at him, but he had a lovely temperament and was great with kids. He'd come from the cat and dog home when he was a wee pup and everyone in the family loved him.

He had this big obsession with getting out of the house every day. He'd practically tear the door down trying to get out and then he'd run off down the stairs and away down the road. My aunt followed him once and witnessed him carefully crossing the road only when there was a human in front of him, then taking a few turns and ending up at the central railway station, which was only two blocks from the house. He sat down on the platform as if he was waiting for something or somebody, and that's what he did all day, every day! He had my aunt's name and number on his collar and sometimes someone'd phone and ask her to come and collect him, but on the whole nobody minded him and he was left to mind his own business on the platform by the ticket office.

Whiskey was well fed at home and nobody at the station gave him treats, so we were mystified as to why he did it. He even ignored all the travellers and the station staff – the only person he took to was a tramp called Frank and he'd make a fuss when he saw him and wag his tail. It wasn't just the central station either – sometimes he'd take a walk round the corner to Queen Street station and wait there. Maybe he just liked trains!

One day we opened up the local newspaper, the Sunday Post, to find a photo of ugly old Whiskey with the headline 'The Station Pooch' with a story all about this 'mysterious' dog who waited at the central station. Was he waiting for his owner to come home on the train from Edinburgh, the journalist speculated, or was he perhaps the reincarnation of a railway guard? People were calling him a modern-day Greyfriars Bobby. 'The Lonely Vigil of the Station Pooch'! We couldn't stop laughing – what a load of nonsense!

I was only a wee girl when this happened, but we all thought it was hysterical. I don't know why Whiskey used to trot off to the station, but he did it rain, wind or snow until right up near the end when he was an old dog and my aunt used to have to keep him on a lead to stop him rushing off on his own to watch the trains.

Was old Whiskey waiting for a previous owner? Maybe. He might just have really liked trains, though! He also could have been looking for someone who was part of his soul group but not yet enlightened enough to recognize him.

It's the nature of reincarnation that consciousness refines and grows because of each physical life that has been lived. All life on this planet has consciousness of sorts and all life has a journey to come through, from the start of its latest incarnation to the so-called death. We all have to learn from our experiences and grow spiritually because of them. If our beloved pets have an emotional experience, good or bad, then they will hopefully learn from it. If they experience a loving connection with a human being, then, like people, they will form a bond that will keep them linked through this life and beyond. That's where soul groups come in.

Millions of people in this world believe we live many lives connected to specific souls that we have bonded with and travel through our lives with, crossing paths time and time again. And it doesn't matter what physical form these souls take from life to life – monk, sheepdog or show horse!

Soul groups have their own purpose, which makes them greater than any individual in them. The ultimate intention of any soul group is for the members to teach one another emotional lessons in order to refine the whole group and take it to a higher level of spirit. Whether your lessons are learned from an animal or a human being, as long as you accept them and understand them, then everyone in your group will be lifted to a greater state of wisdom and each teaching will lead to clarity.

Animals like Charlie come into our lives in a way that affects us profoundly because they've taught us something true and they are in our emotional soul group. Loving companions, compassionate teachers, they are true friends who may share many lives with us.

CHAPTER ELEVEN

~

Charlie

In December 2005, about two years after Charlie had injured his spine, I had a strange dream one night when I was travelling in America. It was one of those dreams that's completely out of the ordinary and stays with you long after you've woken. In it I was up in our house outside Glasgow, standing behind the big window in the living room, when a huge owl flew straight through it. It didn't break the glass, so I remember thinking, 'This must be a spirit bird.' Outside, in the garden, Lassie was just standing under the branches of the pine tree, watching. The owl seized Charlie and flew back out of the window, soaring away with the dog in its talons, although I had the sense that he wasn't hurt at all by the bird. Lassie didn't move. It was disturbing, but I wasn't left feeling frightened or anxious. I thought, 'Why would I see that? What's that about?'

I got back from the States and settled back into my Scottish life and didn't give the dream a second thought. The dogs were on good form and enjoying life. Then I was sitting in the kitchen with Dronma one day and she looked at Charlie and said, 'He's very tired.' He'd been running around on the hills with Meg all morning and he was getting on a bit, so I wasn't that surprised, but something in her tone of voice made me check him carefully. Charlie wasn't just conked out on the floor, he was panting hard. He hadn't gulped up lots of water the way he usually did when he was back from a run. 'Are you OK, Charlie?' Dronma asked and just then a little trickle of blood ran out of his nostril. I didn't need to see any more. We took him to the vet who'd been treating him for years and knew him well.

She didn't like what she saw and kept him in overnight for more tests. The next day Jim and I went back, feeling as though we were about to be sentenced. Jim waited in the car with Meg and I went in alone. The vet welcomed me in and there was Charlie on the examining table, flat on his side. He didn't even wag his tail when he saw me. He looked exhausted.

The vet was frowning. 'How's your other dog?'

'Meg's fine,' I said.

'No vomiting? Not tired?'

'Nothing like that. Why do you ask?'

'Well, it's a strange thing. I don't really have an explanation, but do you know if Charlie might have eaten lots of contraceptive pills?'

I was dumbfounded. 'No, I don't know where he would have got those from.'

'You haven't had any guests who might have had them or been out for a walk anywhere where he could have found lots of packets?'

This was truly bizarre, and I assured her we hadn't had any guests and lately Charlie had only been walking on the hillside behind our village, and no one would have dumped stuff up there. Everyone in the area had dogs, so no one would want to put them at risk. Even if someone had put down rat poison they would have let us all know. There weren't even any farmers locally. What on earth was the matter with him?

The vet went on, 'Well, he's full of oestrogen and I've just never heard of a case like it. He would have had to have eaten packets and packets of pills to have got like this and how would a dog get pills out of a packet? It's the wildest theory I've had and it just doesn't make sense. Also, we've tried to track what is in his stomach but haven't seen any traces of pills or anything like that. So it could be that he's just producing his own oestrogen.'

This was completely strange – as though some female side of Charlie was killing off the male. I must have looked mystified, and the vet was too.

'I've genuinely never seen a male dog producing female hormones like this,' she said. 'I've been on the phone to colleagues all round the country and I've come up blank. None of them has heard of it or seen anything like it. It's as though he has a human form of leukaemia – a human *female* form of leukaemia.'

'Is there any way to be sure?' I was picturing all kinds of treatments and healings that Charlie could have.

The vet sighed again and broke the news gently. 'I could do a lumbar puncture, but this dog is very, very sick. There's no medication, no chemo that's going to help him. Whatever this cancer is, it's running right through him and he'll be dead by tomorrow of his own accord if we don't do something now. He's got no strength left. You can't really want to put him through that procedure. You really have to let me put him down.'

I looked at Charlie who, apart from the constant panting, was lying very still indeed. He looked miserable, his sides heaving, his coat dull. The vet told me that despite being in a cage at the surgery he'd been asleep the whole time. Normally he hated being cooped up, but it seemed that he didn't have the energy to care. Maybe he didn't even recognize where he was. It was hard to believe that just the day before he'd been chasing up the hillsides with Meg, plunging in and out of the bracken with his bunny hop. Now he wasn't the same Cheeky Charlie who'd been part of our family for years, stealing our cigarettes and letting us know who was boss while still comforting the people who came for readings.

I'd already known before we reached the surgery that we might have to let him go; when he'd severed his spine we'd faced the same dilemma, but this time we knew something was different. There was no Tibetan medicine from Dronma that would cure this. Charlie had taken on a lot of karma in his life. He'd known abuse and cruelty. He'd had to come to trust us. He'd been very ill many times and always pulled through. But this was one thing he couldn't beat.

Jim said his goodbyes to our old friend and then went out to the car to sit with Meg. He didn't want to hold Charlie back by being too emotional and upsetting our pet – it would be easier for the dog to slip away if he wasn't reacting to Jim's distress.

I asked the vet for a minute or two and bent down to Charlie's ear and then I started to tell him about all the times he'd run amok in the flat, the times he'd stolen my cigarettes or eaten all the chocolates, or wrecked the house and left me running around trying to cover up the damage before Jim got home – a kind of brief history of the mischief of Charlie. He listened and watched me, but didn't move.

Finally I said, 'Now, Charlie, you rascal, do you remember that time you ate my boots? You got away with it that time!' and there it was: a shot of the old Charlie. He looked at me with a ghost of that old cheekiness in him and his backside trembled and his tail wagged – only a tiny bit, very limply, but it was still a wag. I wanted his last memory to be joyful, and it was. That was the last thing he did.

A minute later the vet said to me, 'You're very together at this point,' and I shrugged and said, 'Well, you've got to be. He's had a good life and he's going to a good place – I know that. He's done well.' Then I turned and left the surgery and went out to the car, but as soon as I saw Meg next to Jim on the front seat with her ears pricked, waiting for Charlie, I blubbed like a kid.

That's when I remembered the dream about the owl and something else Dronma had told me, how in the Apache mythology owls are symbolic of death and often an ill omen. I'd had no idea when I woke from the dream, but Lassie had been giving me an early warning once more – Charlie was going to pass, but it would all be all right.

About three weeks after Charlie died, I dreamed that he was with us again and it felt totally real. There he was, just like his old self, only a few feet away. I wanted him back more than anything – the last few weeks had been very hard. Jim missed him; Meg missed him and had gone looking for him round the house and garden, her head down. They'd been great companions – partners in crime.

I missed him too. He'd been a part of our lives for so long.

In the dream I reached out to him and tried to call to him so he'd run over and have a pat and his belly rubbed, but as I did, a swarm of wasps appeared between me and the dog, buzzing angrily. There was no way I could get to the spaniel.

When I woke up I wondered what it had all meant and later that morning Dronma phoned. 'Did you get the wasps?' she asked.

'The wasps? How did you know about them?'

'Oh, good,' she said. 'This is the third week of Charlie's bardo – you know that's what Tibetan Buddhists call the transitional state between life and death. It's when those left behind miss the one who's passed the most and I knew you would be pining for him so I sent the wasps to warn you off. He'll reach a purer light because you let him go.'

A few months after Charlie died, I went up to the house I'd just left. There were still a few bits and bobs there, but nothing I could really take down to London – a couple of photos, an armchair. I was exhausted – I didn't know whether I was coming or going and moving house had been really stressful. Leaving Scotland, where I'd lived all my life, was weird. I sat down in the chair and began to drift off, looking out at the loch.

Then I could hear Charlie walking across the floor, his claws clicking on the boards, and I felt him push his head up under my hand. I'd done a sending, which is basically the act of letting the animal go and encouraging their consciousness to go to a higher realm rather than keeping them tied to a person on the Earth plane, but here he was, back to see me. In my head I heard myself saying, 'OK, Charlie, I've come to get you and take you home with me,' and I looked up and expected to see him there but he wasn't. I went into the next room and there was a photo of him sitting up and looking proud. How had we forgotten it? I picked it up and took it with me back to London, telling Jim I'd had an amazing experience. It was the first time I'd really felt Charlie's spirit since he'd died and I'd felt how calm he was, beautifully calm.

Later we moved for a second time in London and on 22 December 2007 I had a painter round to put some finishing touches to the walls of our new home before we had Jim's sisters Marie and Elaine to stay for Christmas. I was rushing around trying to get everything sorted when the man came into the kitchen with a puzzled expression on his face. He'd been having a great time making a fuss of Meg and she'd been lying there watching him work and wondering when he'd take a break and throw her ball for her or something. I asked him if he wanted a cup of tea or if I could help him with anything.

'Do you have two of those dogs?' he asked.

'No, just the one.'

He turned pale, 'Don't say that. You're freaking me out now!' He didn't know I was a medium or anything like that.

'Well,' I said, 'we *did* have another dog...'

'Don't!' he said. 'Don't tell me any more! There were two dogs – the little one lying down and another one sitting next to her. It was moving and everything. Oh, this is freaky.'

The poor guy was really stressed out. I knew it must be Charlie, just popping in to see who was in the house. At least he hadn't stolen the man's paintbrushes!

I was so busy that I didn't really think too much about it until the next day when Marie and Elaine arrived. Meg gave them her usual ecstatic greeting and that evening when we were all sitting round having a drink and a chat she did something very strange. Charlie had had a trick he always did for Jim's sisters. He'd lie on his back with his ball in his mouth, somehow flip it up in the air and then jump up into a sitting position and catch it as it fell. Meg always tried to copy him, but she couldn't do it – she wouldn't sit up in time or the ball would go flying off or something. That night she did the trick perfectly and we all applauded. She's never done it since.

Marie was just going off to bed when she said, 'Oh! It was just like there was a dog running by me there. Meg went that way and the dog went the other. How strange.'

She's not the type to believe in spirits, but she was very certain of what she'd sensed. When I said it was probably Charlie, she agreed. 'He's just here for Christmas, then?'

Perhaps he'd come to check out the chocolates under the tree. Then I remembered that 23 December had been the day he had passed two years before.

Every now and again I will do a trance session and let one of my spirit teachers come through and speak. We had a young student once who was stuck with his development and in need of advice, and Dominica came through and started giving him answers to his questions. I wrote a little about Dominica in *Spirit Messenger*. She was a French woman who lived in a convent in San Sebastian in the Basque country some time in the fifteenth century, and she comes through to teach, but only when she judges that she's truly needed.

While Dominica was speaking through me, Meg was getting jumpy and excited. The next thing I knew, my arm was moving out to the side and I was very aware that Dominica was communicating with Meg on a different level. I made a slight motion with my hand, and Meg sat still, unable to move, though her legs were practically vibrating with the need to run around. The young man couldn't believe what he was seeing – it was almost as though a force field had gone up in front of her. Then my fingers moved in a circle and Meg moved in a circle into her bed and just lay there. Later, the student told me he'd been wondering if controlling her like that was right.

Dominica's answer came through, 'Don't worry, I've got Mr Dog here for her' – she always called Charlie 'Mr Dog' and Meg 'Mrs Dog' – 'I've brought Mr Dog to sit with her and keep her company.'

It would have been distracting for Meg to interrupt the trance, so Dominica had found a way to keep her happy.

After that Meg just sat there as if she was totally at peace, and at the end of the session she stood up and waited, as though her paws were behind a line, until the spirit moved away from me, and as soon as that happened she leapt into my lap and started licking me.

It's not that we're hanging on to Charlie and trying to drag him back when he trots through our flat or comes to keep Meg company, it's just that the love we have is still a connection and that bond won't break. I'd never call him to me in a million years, but he might like to cross back. There's a different law on the other side and they can come back when they wish to. Charlie comes when I've been stressed

— being a faithful friend, he notices what's happening and comes because he can. And I know that whatever level of refinement his consciousness reaches, he'll still be there in us, forever Charlie.

You can't love that deeply and learn so much and not have it last.

CHAPTER TWELVE

Soul Companions

Some animals come into the world with a very refined consciousness, though they're always more limited than humans in the way they can display it.

These animals are the ones that stand out to us because there's something they do, like Charlie and his understanding of the circle, or Timone helping someone in need, or Patch with his 'social work' of visiting his elderly human friends, that makes us think, 'Wow, that's a really intelligent animal. He's almost human.' That's not actually true: intelligence is something else altogether. What we're seeing is an animal with highly developed consciousness and compassion.

When we find a beloved pet like this, feelings run deep. How many people have said in this book, 'This was no ordinary dog/cat/horse – I've never known an animal like that'? Magical things happen when you're close to an animal like that, and it's the strength of that bond that lets the extraordinary happen too – the telepathy, the messages from the other side.

Is it so ridiculous to think that a person and animal can be so bonded that they respond to each other as human soulmates would? When you think of the number of people you'll meet in the course of your life and how very few of them will stand out and become friends in the strongest sense, you can see how special such a bond is. The 'owners' in this book all experienced it with those outstanding animals who were surely part of their soul group.

I don't think Charlie could ever have meant the same to his breeder, or his earlier owners, or even the lady who rescued him, as he did to me and Jim. And yet all those adventures, those lessons, all the agonies with his illnesses and injuries, all the times when he made us laugh or made us think and look at our own assumptions and behaviour, all those were just waiting to happen for the right person.

There's a story about a Brahmin called Kukku Ripa who lived in India, centuries ago. He was travelling alone, having renounced the world, and was living on the charity that people in the villages he passed through dropped into his begging bowl. One day he was trudging on to the next town when he heard a noise from the roadside, and when he went to look he found a starving young dog. He couldn't leave her there, but carried her on with him, sharing his food with her until she recovered and could walk alongside him.

After much journeying with the dog as his constant companion, he reached the caves of Lumbini in Nepal, where he intended to stay and meditate on his way to enlightenment. For 12 years he recited his mantra, leaving the cave only to fetch food for himself and the dog, who stood guard at the cave's mouth while he was away.

The gods of the 33 sensual heavens saw what he had achieved on Earth and how close he was to divine insight, and they invited him to come and celebrate with them in their paradise. Kukku Ripa ascended to join them and found a magical place where there was always feasting and luxury.

The dog waited on Earth, and even when he was all but lost in his heavenly new existence, Kukku Ripa didn't forget her. In fact, he missed her and he could see that she was pining for him. He begged the gods to let him return to her. Baffled, they finally agreed.

When Kukku Ripa arrived back at the cave mouth, the dog was ecstatic, and as he leaned down to tickle her under her ears, she suddenly disappeared and was replaced by a beautiful *dakini* – a goddess. She told Kukku Ripa that by overcoming the temptations of the 33 heavens and coming back for his friend, he had proved himself fit to achieve supreme realization.

Ultimately, being good for the sake of being a good Brahmin wasn't enough, and Kukku Ripa found that he truly received grace only when he reached out to someone that needed his help – and that could have been a dog, a cow or another person. In feeling love for that animal, that man became enlightened – a compassionate, loving individual, not an ascetic saint.

We can all see ourselves as individuals or we can realize we're part of a bigger consciousness and try to reach out for an unconditional love of all beings.

If you've felt moved reading about Carole and Sassy the Yorkie, or Philippa and Boyzie, or the way Zizikos turned to Eleni when he was in trouble, then you already know what I'm talking about and you're already on the road to understanding that we can all find that bond in our lives.

The essence of love, of those bonds, that runs through our lives, is what gives us meaning. No matter whom we feel love for in this life, human or animal, the very fact that we have loved another being will expand who we are and give us a higher perspective. All animals can touch our hearts if we let them.

ABOUT THE AUTHOR

Gordon Smith is hailed as 'the UK's best medium', renowned for his astonishing ability to pinpoint exact names of people, places and even streets relevant to a person's life.

From early childhood, Gordon had the ability to see, sense and hear spirit people. At the age of 24, he embarked on 15 years of study and practice, going on to develop his abilities as a medium – or messenger from the spirit world – under the tutelage of some of the great legends of the spiritualist church.

Gordon is now a bestselling author and one of the world's top psychic mediums and spiritual teachers, conducting mediumship workshops and events around the world. His Celtic charm and lively demonstrations – delivered in his trademark style combining humour, pure passion and empathy towards others – provide his audiences with a rare opportunity to experience the fascinating phenomenon of mediumship.

www.gordonsmithmedium.com

HAY HOUSE
Look within

Join the conversation about latest products,
events, exclusive offers and more.

 Hay House UK

 @HayHouseUK

 @hayhouseuk

 healyourlife.com

We'd love to hear from you!

Printed in the United States
by Baker & Taylor Publisher Services